About the Author

Abbas Panakkal is a historian currently affiliated with the School of History at the University of St Andrews, United Kingdom. Simultaneously, he holds a position on the advisory board at the Religious Life and Belief Centre, University of Surrey, United Kingdom. Panakkal is engrossed in an ongoing research project that explores the intricate dynamics of integration and indigenization of vernacular communities. His scholarly prowess is evident through his editorial contributions to several impactful volumes, including *South Asian Islam: A Spectrum of Integration and Indigenization* (2023), *Matrilineal, Matriarchal, and Matrifocal Islam: The World of Women-centric Islam* (2024) and *Southeast Asian Islam: Integration and Indigenization* (2024). In recognition of his dedication to fostering interfaith understanding, Panakkal serves as the director of the International Interfaith Harmony Initiative. This role has seen him play a pivotal part in organizing international interfaith conferences, collaborating with esteemed entities such as the United Nations Interfaith Initiatives, the Malaysian Prime Minister's Department of National Unity and Integration and the International Islamic University Malaysia for over a decade. Adding to his academic accolades, Panakkal has been honored with a research fellowship by Griffith University in Australia. His broad-ranging research covers diverse subjects, including language, religion, integration, indigenization and regions such as South Asia and Southeast Asia.

ADVAITA VEDĀNTA
An Introduction

ARVIND SHARMA

MOTILAL BANARSIDASS PUBLISHERS
PRIVATE LIMITED • DELHI

First Edition: Delhi, 2004

ISBN: 81-208-2027-4

Also available at:

MOTILAL BANARSIDASS
41 U.A. Bungalow Road, Jawahar Nagar, Delhi 110 007
8 Mahalaxmi Chamber, 22 Bhulabhai Desai Road, Mumbai 400 026
120 Royapettah High Road, Mylapore, Chennai 600 004
236, 9th Main III Block, Jayanagar, Bangalore 560 011
Sanas Plaza, 1302 Baji Rao Road, Pune 411 002
8 Camac Street, Kolkata 700 017
Ashok Rajpath, Patna 800 004
Chowk, Varanasi 221 001

Printed in India
BY JAINENDRA PRAKASH JAIN AT SHRI JAINENDRA PRESS,
A-45 NARAINA, PHASE-I, NEW DELHI 110 028
AND PUBLISHED BY NARENDRA PRAKASH JAIN FOR
MOTILAL BANARSIDASS PUBLISHERS PRIVATE LIMITED,
BUNGALOW ROAD, DELHI 110 007

Contents

Preface

The Biblical recognition of the fact that to the writing of books there is no end must surely not be used as an excuse for writing books indiscriminately. The readers therefore have a right to ask : why another book on Advaita Vedānta?

Most of the existing books on Advaita Vedānta rely on the *scriptural* approach in presenting it. Some books mix it with the *rational* and *experiential* approaches as well, without always distinguishing clearly between them. This book tries to accord an independent status to each of these approaches without losing sight of their interconnectedness in the hope that the readers will find such a presentation refreshing.

I hope that this pedagogical variation in the way Advaita Vedānta is thematically presented will be welcomed by the readers.

—Arvind Sharma

INTRODUCTION

Religion, Philosophy and Advaita Vedānta

I. Religion and Philosophy in India and the West

It might be helpful to say a few words about the nature of philosophy as it is pursued in India, prior to providing an introduction to the school of Indian philosophy known as Advaita Vedānta.

Both Western and Indian philosophers admit that the nature of the relationship between philosophy and religion follows a different pattern in Western and Indian civilization but they tend to differ in their assessment of the significance of this divergence. Both accept that philosophy essentially consists of a rational investigation into the nature of Reality. The nature of the Reality, however, also constitutes, in its own way, the subject matter of religion, so the nature of the relationship between the two needs to be considered.

A relationship between religion and philosophy is considered peripheral in Western culture for historical and philosophical reasons. In the West, philosophy represents an intellectual movement which first distinguished itself from theology and then proceeded to achieve an independent status. This meant that the attitude of Western philosophy towards religion came to be marked by indifference, aversion and perhaps even rejection. Such a development did not occur within Indian culture. Thus, although the distinction between philosophy and religion can also be drawn in the Indian context, such a distinction therein tends to be analytical without being antagonistic. It can even be claimed that the two, even when they become dual, remain undivided. Moreover, the distinction between philosophy and religion in the West additionally rests on the distinction between reason and faith, with reason constituting the cornerstone of philosophy and faith that of religion. This distinction is strengthened by the fact that the results of faith are typically accessible only posthumously, while the results of rational investigation are typically available here and now.

A separation of philosophy and religion is intellectually approved of in the West, as this allows for the pursuit of philosophical truths untrammelled by religious scruples. Many Indian thinkers, however, take a different view of the matter. According to them this divorce of philosophy from religion runs the risk of reducing philosophy to a merely intellectual pastime, far removed from the kind of ultimate concern which should ideally characterise philosophy. In this context they make a further point: that although the claims made by Indian philosophy may sometimes seem to possess a religious nature, they are attainable within this life, and are therefore, in principle, verifiable.

The successful attainment of such results is characterised by the term *jīvanmukti*. Not all schools of either Indian philosophy, or of Hindu philosophy, make such a claim but Advaita Vedānta does[1]—along with the Hindu systems of Sāṅkhya and Yoga. The claim also characterises much of Buddhist and Jaina thought. The term *jīvanmukti* is often translated as *living liberation*, as the word *mukti* means *liberation* and *jīvan* means *while living*. The idea underlying *jīvanmukti* thus seems to be that one can attain the results of one's *faith* while still living in this world. There is no reason in principle why faith in *reason* could not also represent such faith.

These ideas contrast, perhaps even sharply, with those found in the thought of other religious systems such as those of Christianity and Islam. In Christianity and Islam, specifically in their more traditional versions of Catholicism and Sunni Islam, the benefits of faith are to be enjoyed in a post-mortem existence. That is to say, one does not experience the results of one's faith until after death, or perhaps not even until the Day of Judgement, which takes place not at the time of one's death but at the end of the world or of Time itself. This leads to the curious situation that one of the questions critically debated in those traditions which accept *jīvanmukti* is "What happens to the liberated one after his or her death" rather than "What happens after death"! The grand question is not what happens after death as in Christianity and Islam, but what happens to the liberated person after his or her death.

It is clear that the concept of *faith* itself also carries very different connotations in the schools which accept *jīvanmukti*, compared with those of the West. In schools which accept *jīvanmukti*, faith is understood as *faith pending realization* - it denotes the trust one must have in order to undertake an experiment, but the outcome of the experiment is independent of such faith. It is even possible that the revealed results might contribute towards strengthening faith, just as one's faith in science is strengthened when one experimentally discovers that water is made of two gases.

It is in the light of these considerations that Indian thinkers take a more positive view of the fact that philosophy and religion have not been *sundered* in India, as in the West. This attitude is also reflected in their treatment of Advaita Vedānta.

To recapitulate: Philosophy in the Western world consists of rational investigation into the nature of reality. For Indian philosophers, however, philosophy in the Western world is only half of what it should be. They like to say that Western philosophy is a purely intellectual activity, and that in the West religion and philosophy have been broken apart. In the West, then, reason is opposed to faith. This split, they argue, has not occurred in the Indian tradition. Thus many schools of thought in the Indian religious traditions feel no awkwardness, embarrassment or self-consciousness in discussing the ultimate nature of reality *both* from a philosophical *and* a religious perspective. Advaita Vedānta is one such school.

II. Advaita Vedānta and other Schools of Indian Thought

Since religion cannot be completely overlooked when dealing with philosophy in the Indian context, it is useful to draw a distinction between Indian religions and Indic religions. The term Indian religions refers to all the religions found in India such as Hinduism, Buddhism, Jainism, Sikhism, Judaism, Zoroastrianism, Christianity, Islam and so on. The term Indic religions, by contrast, is used to refer only to the religions of Indian origin collectively, namely Hinduism, Buddhism, Jainism and Sikhism. Indian philosophy, again by contrast, is classically taken to refer to the philosophical systems which characterise the *Indic* religions.

In one classification, which has gained wide acceptance since 1900 when it was adopted by Max Mueller, Indian philosophy includes nine schools of Indian thought.[2] A school of philosophy in India known as *darśana*, a word which may be translated in several ways. It is derived from the verbal root which means *to see*, thereby yielding such meanings as *insights into reality* or *worldviews*. These nine systems are further classified into the non-orthodox and orthodox systems of Indian thought as follows:

Indian Philosophy (*Darśana*)	
Non-Orthodox schools of Hindu thought *Nāstika* (3) Indian Materialism Buddhism Jainism	Orthodox Schools of Hindu thought *Āstika* (6) Nyāya Vaiśeṣika Sāṅkhya Yoga Mīmāṁsā Vedānta

Asti in the word *āstika* above means *yes* and *na* in the word *nāstika* changes the meaning into *no*. The three non-orthodox schools of Indic thought do not accept Vedic authority; to be *nāstika* is to say no to the Vedas. *Āstika*, then, means saying yes to the Vedas. Among the six schools which accept Vedic authority, the first four, that is Nyāya, Vaiśeṣika, Sāṅkhya and Yoga, indeed accept the authority of the Vedas but they do so basically *a posteriori* rather than *a priori*. The last two schools of Mīmāṁsā and Vedānta, however, actually base themselves on the Vedas.

It is obvious that orthodoxy here has been defined from a Hindu perspective, and the acceptance of the authority of the Vedas, the foundational scriptures of Hinduism, has been identified as its hallmark. It should now be added that the Mīmāṁsā and Vedānta schools are to be further distinguished from the above-mentioned *āstika* schools in that they not only acknowledge the authority of, but also base their teachings on the Vedas. Therefore, in order to understand these schools, it is important to understand the traditional view of the Vedas.

The term *Veda* comes from the root *vid*, which means *to know*, as in *video* (to know visually). The Vedas are said to have been revealed to or *seen* by the sages. It is traditionally understood that the Vedas are not works of human authors. This idea also exists in the Islamic tradition, where the Qur'ān is understood to have been *received* by the Prophet Muhammad from God. In Hindu Vedantic thought, however, even God is eliminated as the author. The Vedas are woven into the fabric and texture of the universe, which is eternal. This in turn means that the Vedas are eternal, and are periodically *discovered*, and not created or invented.

The Vedas have never been formalised into a closed canon, although a certain degree of informal consensus does exist. This uncertainty has the subtle effect of making the person who speaks with authority more influential than the text. Because the Vedas are numerous and the canon loosely defined, it stands to reason that one would turn to a person who has experienced *jīvanmukti* for authoritative opinion, rather than sift through a mass of confusing, indeterminate, and sometimes contradictory information.

The Vedas are four in number. Each of the four Vedas (*Ṛg, Sāma, Yajur, Atharva*) can be divided into four different layers, just as the Christian Bible can be divided into two layers, the Old Testament and the New. Judaism and Christianity differ in that they do not accept the same layer as authoritative. In a somewhat similar fashion, Mīmāṁsā thought regards the earlier parts of the Vedas as of primary importance, whereas Vedānta accords greater authority to the last layer, consisting of the Upaniṣads. The Upaniṣads, according to Vedānta, mark the consummation of all the previous layers, and thereby reveal the final truth contained in the Vedas.

The basis of the classification of the *darśanas,* or schools of thought, provided above was textual, the text involved being the Veda. The point however should not be overstated. As already noted, the word *āstika* comes from the verbal root which literally means *to be* or *yes it is*; which means that these schools have responded with a yes to the question: "do you accept the authority of the Vedas?" The six *āstika* schools: Nyāya, Vaiśeṣika, Sāṅkhya, Yoga, Mīmāṁsā and Vedānta were mentioned earlier. It was also mentioned that the first four of these, although they accept Vedic authority, do not base their teaching on the Vedas. These schools simply acknowledge the authority of the Vedas, and then proceed to go on and do what they like. Because the corpus of Vedic scripture is vast, one could justify almost any view, and therefore nominally acknowledge the authority of these texts. Thus acceptance of Vedic authority is not as binding for philosophical purposes as it is for social cohesion. Hence the four schools are listed *before* the two schools of Mīmāṁsā and Vedānta because they accept Vedic authority only nominally and *after* the three non-orthodox schools because nevertheless they do accept it, instead of rejecting the Vedas like the three non-orthodox schools.

III. A Philosophical Explanation of the Classification

It is also possible to provide a more philosophical justification for the nature and order of this system of classification–specially from the perspective of Advaita Vedānta, the subject of our study. This has to do with the concept of the self or *ātman,* which plays such a key role in Advaita Vedānta that the system itself has been referred to as *ātmādvaita.*

One can detect a pattern in the progression of thought through these nine schools, if one examines their concept of the *ātman,* the *self* or *soul.* The materialists believe that natural elements suffice to give rise to consciousness in human beings. As materialism does not acknowledge an *ātman,* the materialists encourage people to live for the moment, for death is final. They believe in happiness through materialism, in keeping with the maxim: "eat, drink and be merry." Buddhism also does not acknowledge an *ātman* but it accepts allied concepts such as a belief in the cycle of rebirth. Jainism accepts an *ātman,* but it is considered coextensive with the physical body. Nyāya and Vaiśeṣika also believe in an *ātman.* However, in these systems although the *ātman* does exist, it cannot exhibit consciousness independently of accessories, that is, by itself. Sāṅkhya and Yoga also believe in an independent *ātman.* But they also posit a strict dualism between matter and spirit, although the two are not on par. Matter is subservient to spirit and all matter is integrated into one category. (In other schools matter, is sometimes split into different ultimate parts.) However, in these systems, all *ātmans* retain their individuality to the very end. They do not merge into one. The concept of *ātman* in Advaita Vedānta, however, unites all entities in the realm of the spirit into Brahman, just as Sāṅkhya and Yoga unite all entities in the realm of matter into *prakṛti.* The school of Advaita Vedānta thus arguably represents a culmination of the underlying philosophical thrust around the concept of the *ātman* or self as found in Indian philosophy.

IV. Another Philosophical Explanation of the Classification

Another philosophical justification of classification can be found in the attitudes of the various schools towards the relationship between the realms of matter and spirit. Both matter and consciousness are equally given in human experience: we see material objects all around us, and it is immaterial consciousness which enables us to be aware of them.

Since both matter and spirit in this sense are empirically given, three fundamental philosophical positions can be postulated on this point: (1) that it is matter alone which is the ultimate reality, consciousness being its epi-phenomenon, a position which may be characterised as materialism, (2) that both matter and spirit constitute ultimate reality in their own right, a position which may be described as that of fundamental dualism (3) or that spirit alone is ultimately real, matter being its byproduct, a position which may be characterised as idealism.

In terms of this schema, the classification of the nine schools starts with materialism, then moves through the fundamentally dualistic schools which accept the reality of both matter and spirit, to end with Vedānta which is idealistic in its orientation, Advaita Vedānta being specially so.

V. Advaita Vedānta: What Does it Mean?

Let us begin with the word *Advaita* itself, which perhaps appears formidably foreign when first encountered. It can however be de-exoticised quite easily with the help of a brief foray into philology. It can be broken up as *a-dvaita.* The initial *a* here has the same meaning as the letter a in ahistorical, that is, of negating what follows. Thus just as ahistorical means *not*-historical, *a-dvaita* means *not*-dvaita.

But what does *dvaita* mean? This word is etymologically connected with the English word dual – a connection which can be phonetically heard if one says the two words *dvaita* and *dual* out aloud. The word *dvaita,* moreover, not only sounds like dual, but shares its meaning as well. Thus *dvaita* means dualism or *twoness.*

The word *advaita* (*a-dvaita*) thus means not-two or non-dual.

The word is however an adjective — so the question arises: what is it being applied to? In other words, what is it about which this claim is being made that it is *not two*?

So let us put the word *advaita* on hold for a moment and try to find out what the word which it qualifies means; namely, *Vedānta*. The two can then be brought together again to reveal their meaning in its fullness.

The word *Vedānta* might also, like the word *advaita*, appear forbiddingly alien at first sight. But once again it yields its meaning easily with the help of a mercifully brief excursion into philology.

The word *Vedānta* is made of two words – *veda* + *anta*. The word *Veda* is derived from a root which means to *know*— the same root which appears in three English words: wit, wisdom and video, that is, to know intelligently (wit); to know sagely (wisdom) and to know visually (video). The word *Veda*, derived from the same root *vid* (to know) as noticed earlier, denotes wisdom, that is to say, *spiritual* wisdom, and by implication the texts which embody such wisdom. Thus it is that the sacred scriptures of the Hindus are called the Vedas, just as the sacred scripture of the Christians is known as the Bible, and of the Muslims as the Qur'ān. Note that unlike the Bible and the Qur'ān, the word Veda often takes a plural ending. This is so because traditionally one speaks of the *four* Vedas, a fact also noticed earlier. Sometimes, however, the word *Veda* is also used in the singular to refer to the Vedas collectively. The fact that, even to begin with, Hinduism possesses four sacred books and not just one tells us something about the inherently plural ethos of the tradition.

Not only are the Vedas four in number, four layers can be identified in each of them. The following chart may help clarify the picture in this respect.

	Vedas			
	Ṛg	*Yajur*	*Sāma*	*Atharva*
Mantra or *Saṁhitā*	—	—	—	—
Brāhmaṇa	—	—	—	—
Āraṇyaka	—	—	—	—
Upaniṣad	—	—	—	—

Each of the Vedas contains (1) hymns (many shared by them in common) in praise of the gods; (2) prose explanations of the ritual use of these hymns; (3) reflections on the significance of ritual and (4) secret texts meant to communicate the highest mysteries which go beyond ritual into the realm of spiritual knowledge. These layers are respectively called (1) *mantra* or *saṁhitā* (i.e. hymns, or collections of hymns); (2) *brāhmaṇa* (i.e. authoritative utterances of priests); (3) *āraṇyakas* (i.e. forest-books) and (4) *upaniṣads* (or mystic texts revealed to disciples as they sat up close to the masters).

The rest of our presentation will focus on the *upaniṣads.* Because they come at the end of the Vedas, or constitute the last of the four layers, they are also called Ved*ānta,* that is, Veda's *end.* The word *anta* in Sanskrit has the same meaning as the English word *end.*

The texts which constitute the *Upaniṣads,* or *Vedānta,* deal with the central issues of philosophy: what is the ultimate reality about the universe around us and about us who are asking this question? And what is the ultimate nature of this ultimate reality?

The *Upaniṣads,* (more than two hundred of which have been identified, among which close to a dozen or more are considered major ones) do not offer, at least on the face of it, a single answer to these questions. They are closer to being works of religious inspiration than systematic treatises on theology, and the inspired statements found therein lend themselves to many interpretations. Thus different schools of philosophy arose in India out of an attempt to present their teachings in a systematic way. These various schools of philosophy are known as schools of Vedānta, and they differ in their interpretation regarding the final teaching of the *Upaniṣads*. Thus questions such as: *is the ultimate reality ultimately personal or impersonal in nature?* are answered differently by these schools. Similarly, the schools differ in the answer they come up with to such questions as: what is the relationship of the ultimate reality (*Brahman*) to the world, or what does Realization consist of.

Advaita Vedānta is one such school of Vedānta. It is labeled *Advaita* because it does not ultimately regard either us or the universe as different from the ultimately reality – they are not-two. It prefers to call them *not-two* rather than *one* because not-two implies a lack of fundamental division to begin with, whereas *one* may imply the coming together of two items that are in fact apart. Hence it prefers to speak in terms of an "undivided" (*a-dvaita*) Reality, in preference to one Reality, because according to it the positing of such a fundamental division is itself a product of error.

Are all living beings ultimately identical with *Brahman*? Is the universe also identical with it? Is there any difference between the way the living beings are identical with *Brahman* compared to the way the universe is? If the ultimate reality is a single undivided Reality, what reality do the different things and different people around us possess? Are they defilements or embellishments, and how can they exist without involving duality on the part of an undivided reality? The school of Advaita Vedānta tries its best to answer these questions by relying (1) on revelation, (2) on reason and (3) on the teachings of those who are said to be living embodiments of the Realization of *Brahman* or the ultimate Reality.

PART I

Advaita Vedānta: A Scriptural Approach

The scriptural approach relies on scriptural authority as the basis for the claims it makes regarding the nature of the ultimate reality. This reality is regularly referred to in the Upaniṣads as *Brahman.*

The Upaniṣads, however, make several pronouncements regarding the nature of the objective world, the nature of the individual subject and the nature of the ultimate reality (*Brahman*), with the result that "there are great, almost insurmountable difficulties in deciding what exactly is the teaching of the Upaniṣads in certain important respects. This accounts for the emergence in later times of diverse schools of Vedānta, all of which claim to propound the Upaniṣadic teaching".[3] It is also worth adding that:

> The vagueness of Upanishadic teaching is particularly in reference to the relation of Brahman to the individual soul on the one hand, and to the physical universe on the other. Though... statements about their identity are many and prominent, those distinguishing them are not altogether wanting. The first problem to solve for any one attempting to systematize the teaching of the Upanishads is accordingly to harmonize these two sets of statements.[4]

Each system of Vedānta has evolved its own method of harmonizing these statements on the underlying assumption (contained in *Brahmasūtra* 1.1.4) that these Upaniṣadic teachings have to be understood in a unified way. Advaita

Vedānta, as a system of Vedānta, has devised its own understanding of the Upaniṣads in keeping with this assumption.

It was noted above that the Upaniṣads seem to contain two streams of thought: one which recognizes the diversity of the objective universe, the subjective individual and the ultimate reality (*Brahman*) and another which emphasizes their unity. The great exponent of Advaita Vedānta :

> Śaṁkara recognizes, that there are two streams of thought in the Upanishads; but he thinks that one of them, viz. that which affirms the reality of diversity, is only a concession to empirical modes of thought. All diversity being thus only conditionally true, the only teaching of the Upanishads, according to him, is that of unity. Since, however, there can be no unity apart from variety, he does not describe his teaching as monism but only as "non-dualism" (*advaita*).[5]

How, it might now be asked, does Śaṅkara achieve such a result?

He achieves this outcome through an exegetical manoeuvre according to which the Upaniṣads are said to contain certain key statements called *mahāvākyas*, and through the subsequent claim that their teachings as a whole are to be understood through the lens of these seminal utterances. It is like claiming that if one wants to understand the New Testament, this is best done in the light of the overarching statement that "Jesus is the Messiah". All other parts of the New Testament which do not directly confirm this—as when Jesus asks Peter: who do you think I am?—or when Jesus wonders on the cross whether God has forsaken him—are all to be understood subject to the *mahāvākya*: "Jesus is the Messiah".

These *mahāvākyas*, in the light of which the Upaniṣads should be understood according to the hermeneutical tradition of Advaita Vedānta, are the following:

I. All this is verily Brahman.
II. I am Brahman.
III. This Ātman is Brahman.
IV. That thou art.

To this a fifth is sometimes added:
V. Brahman is spirit (or consciousness).

These statements, however, need to be understood with extreme exegetical care, for they can be easily misunderstood. Indeed these *mahāvākyas* are accepted as authoritative by other schools of Vedānta as well, so it is not so much the fact of singling out these statements as *mahāvākyas* as their understanding within Advaita Vedānta, which sets this system apart from other schools of Vedānta.[6]

All This is Verily Brahman

The reader will, for instance, note that this first statement identifies the objective universe with *Brahman*. The reader will also note that the second statement (*I am Brahman*) identifies the individual with *Brahman*. However, the exact manner in which the objective universe is held to be identical with the *Brahman*; and the individual subject (or *jīva* is held to be identical with *Brahman*, are *not* identical.

> Before explaining this difference, it is necessary to draw attention to an important distinction between two types of illusion in common experience. A person may fancy that he sees a serpent at a distance, while closer scrutiny reveals to him that it is only a rope. The latter or correcting knowledge, like practically all knowledge of the kind, affirms the existence of something; but it contradicts that object *as which* (i.e., serpent) that something appeared before. He says to himself or feels when he discovers his error: "It is a rope, not a serpent." Again a person looking at a white conch through a sheet of yellow glass, of whose existence he is not aware, takes it

> to be yellow. But a suitable change in his standpoint will disclose to him that the yellowness belongs to the glass and not to the conch. Here also, as in the previous case, the later knowledge affirms the existence of some reality; unlike it, however, it does not deny the object as which it appeared, viz. the conch, but only an *aspect* of it – its yellowness. He still sees it as a conch, but only adds that it is white and not yellow. The illusion in the first case consists in mistaking a given object for another that is not given; in the second, it consists merely in attributing to an object which is given, a feature that does not really belong to it, though it also is presented at the time. But for the interposition of the sheet of glass (*upādhi*) to which the yellow actually belongs, there would be no illusion at all in the latter case. Now these types of illusions serve to illustrate the difference in the manner in which, according to Śaṅkara, one and the same Brahman comes to appear both as the world and as the individual self (*jīva*). It gives rise to the illusion of the world, as the rope does to that of a serpent in the first example.[7]

The relationship of the *jīva* to *Brahman*, however, must be explained with the help of the other example, for the "Jīva is not false or illusory as the world is."[8] Rather it is "its limitations which are false,"[9] and "these limitations, which are really its empirical adjuncts, appeared transferred to it, as in our second example of illusions, the yellowness of the glass appeared transferred to the conch."[10] As a result:

> The ultimate truth, as realised by a *jīvanmukta*, denies the world while affirming the underlying reality of Brahman which is given in all presentations as positive being (*sat*) and with which we may therefore be said to be constantly, though not consciously, in touch. The individual self, on

> the other hand, is not illusory in this sense. It is Brahman itself appearing through media or limiting adjuncts (*upādhi*) like the internal organ (*antaḥkaraṇa*) which, we may state by the way, are all elements pertaining to the physical world and, as such, are illusory. Or, to state the same otherwise, the individual self when seen *sub specie aeternitatis*, is Brahman itself. When this fact is realized in one's own experience, what is denied is not the *jīva* as a spiritual entity, but only certain aspects of it, such as its finitude and its separateness from other selves. Its conception may thereby become profoundly transformed, but the important point is that it is not negated (*bādhita*) in the same way in which the physical world is. It is, on the other hand, reaffirmed, though only as Brahman. We cannot thereby say that the individual self is false (*mithyā*), as we may that the world is false. We can only say that it is not truly the agent, the enjoyer, etc.[11]

The overall picture which emerges on the basis of this discussion may be presented succinctly as follows:

> We now know the advaitic world-view in general. Brahman is the sole reality, and it appears both as the objective universe and as the individual subject. The former is an illusory manifestation of Brahman, while the latter is Brahman itself appearing under the limitations which form part of that illusory universe.[12]

I am Brahman

The second statement, "I am Brahman" must now be examined in more detail. The subjective individual – the *I* – is regularly referred to in Advaita as the *jīvātman*, or *jīva* for short. The importance of this compound form will become clear at the end of this exposition, although the term *jīvātman* will be referred to as *jīva* during the exposition for the sake of brevity.

In the case of the distinction between the first two *mahāvākyas*—one which identified the *Brahman* with the universe and the other which identified it with the *jīva*—it turned out to be the case that although both were said to be identical with *Brahman*, the exact nature of this identity was not identical. The clue to the understanding of the second *mahāvākya* and the kind of identity it involves is provided by the fact that although the *jīva* is referred to as *anādi*, or beginningless, from both an empirical and a transcendental point of view, this "beginninglessness" in the two cases is not identical in nature.

It was noted earlier that the notion of the *jīva* is "that of a complex (*viśiṣṭa*), and points not only to an element which is identical with Brahman, but also to limiting adjuncts like the internal organs."[13] It is important to keep this in mind as we proceed. The empirical reality about the *jīva* consists of the fact that it is caught up in the process of *saṁsāra*, bound by its *karma*, or actions.

> Here no doubt, a question will be asked as to when the responsibility for what one does *first* occurred. But such a question is really inadmissible, for it takes for granted that there was a time when the self was without any disposition whatsoever. Such a view of the self is an abstraction as meaningless as that of mere disposition which characterises no one. The self, as ordinarily known to us, always means a self with a certain stock of dispositions; and this fact is indicated in Indian expositions by describing karma as beginningless (*anādi*). It means that no matter how far back we trace the history of an individual, we shall never arrive at a stage when he was devoid of all character.[14]

This is one sense in which the *jīva* is *anādi*, or beginningless. The other sense in which it is *anādi*, or beginningless, may be identified by asking the question: does the *jīva, in its true nature,* undergo any change in the process of being involved in the universe? In this context:

> It is desirable to distinguish further between actual and apparent change. Actual change (*pariṇāma*) signifies that when a particular thing is destroyed, it does not disappear entirely. A rope when pulled to pieces remains as fibres. A pot, when broken, exists as potsherds. In apparent transformation (*vivarta*), on the other hand, the disappearance is complete. When the illusion of "serpent" is overcome, there will be nothing of *it* left. It remains only to add that the *jīva* is not an effect in either of these senses. It is not a real transformation, nor even an illusory appearance of Brahman, so that no principle of causation is at all involved there. If we yet speak of the individual self as born, we only mean that its adjuncts like the physical body come into being and not the spiritual element in it. Hence the *jīva* is described as beginningless (*anādi*). It is, as already indicated, Brahman appearing in an empirical dress.[15]

The distinction between the nature of this example with the one cited earlier should be noted. In the first example the difference between the two illusions—of the rope-snake and tinted-conch—consisted of the fact that while in the case of the rope-snake, what is not given at all (snake) was taken as given, in the case of the tinted-conch, only a feature of the conch, the yellow-tint was taken as given when not given. The conch as such is given forever, and because it is given *for ever,* no concept of change, whether apparent or actual, applies to it. It is not the argument that the white conch was transformed into a yellow conch and when the error was discovered, was transformed back into a white conch, when the yellow colour *was removed.* The yellow colour was never part of the conch.

Anything which is beginninglessness is assumed under normal philosophical assumptions to be endless, i.e. eternal. So we discover that the *jīva* is eternal in *two* senses: (1) It is eternal in the sense that it is part of *saṁsāra* which, as a process is eternal, (2) it is *eternal* in the sense that it is identical with *Brahman*, which is eternal. It is perhaps because it is eternal in *both* the senses that it can be referred to as *jīvātman*. As the permanently still witness to its eternally fluctuating fortunes the *jīvātman* is known as the *sākṣī* or witness; the permanent as the witness of the constant.

But this leads to the view that there can be two kinds of eternalities. Such indeed is the case.

> In Indian philosophy two kinds of eternity are distinguished, a) *kūṭastha nityatā* and b) *pravāharūpa nityatā*. A thing is *kūṭastha nitya* if it is unchanged forever, while a thing is *pravāharūpa nitya* if though incessantly changing it does not alter its pattern (*niyati*). Roughly speaking, a rock, for example, has the former kind of reality, and a river the latter kind. The nature of a river is to flow incessantly, and so long as it does not swerve from this nature of its, it may be said to be *mutably real*; though not *enduringly real* as a rock.[16]

The *jīva* part of *jīvātman* partakes of *pravāharūpa-nityatā*, and the ātman element in it partakes of *kūṭastha-nityatā*.

Thus when it is said that "I am Brahman", it is not the *jīva* but the *ātman* element of the complex which is referred to. Be it also noted that the statement "aham brahma asmi," (*I am Brahman*) while it may lead to the conviction that all spirit is one, "leaves out of account the entire physical universe"[17], thereby indicating the importance of the first *mahāvākya*.

Ātman is Brahman

We turn now to the third *mahāvākya*: that ātman is *Brahman*.

One may begin by recognizing the importance of this identification in the light of Vedic and Upaniṣadic literature. M. Hiriyanna writes:

> Thus Brahman means the eternal principle as realized in the world as a whole; and ātman, the inmost essence of one's own self. These two conceptions—Brahman and ātman—are of great importance and occur not only independently in the literature of this period, but are sometimes corelated with each other; and their parallelism is pointed out by representing the self of the world as related to the physical universe in the same manner in which the individual self is related to the body. Thus in Atharva Veda, the universal self or world-soul is stated to have "the earth for its feet, the atmospheric region for its belly, the sky for its head, the sun and moon for its eyes and the wind for its breath."[18]

He then goes on to say:

> The two conceptions are also sometimes identified; and it is this happy identification of them that constitutes the essential teaching of the Upanishads. They mean that the principle underlying the world as a whole, and that which forms the essence of man, are ultimately the same. Here ended the long Indian quest for the pervasive cause of all things—the search, as the Upanishads express it, for "that by knowing which all will be known." Passages descriptive of Brahman alone or of ātman alone occur frequently in the Upanishads; but they are not peculiar to them, being also found in the earlier literature. Their explicit identification, on the other hand, is specifically Upanishadic.[19]

What, however, is the philosophical importance of this identification apart from its textual significance?

The answer to this question is best provided by the perspective that the search for the ultimate reality in the Upaniṣads followed two routes: an external route and an internal route. The external approach was represented by the search for the ultimate ground of the external universe. The following passage from the Upaniṣads provides a glimpse of such an approach in operation:

The regressus to Brahma, the ultimate world-ground.

Then Gārgī Vācaknavī questioned him. *Yajñavalkya,* said she, *since all this world is woven, warp and woof, on water, on what, pray, is the water woven, warp and woof?*

'On wind, O Gārgī.'

'On what then, pray, is the wind woven, warp and woof?'

'On the atmosphere-worlds, O Gārgī.'

'On what then, pray, are the atmosphere-worlds woven, warp and woof?'

'On the worlds of the Gandharvas, O Gārgī.'

'On what then, pray, are the worlds of the Gandharvas woven, warp and woof?'

'On the worlds of the sun, O Gārgī.'

'On what then, pray, are the worlds of the sun woven, warp and woof?'

'On the worlds of the moon, O Gārgī.'

'On what then, pray, are the worlds of the moon woven, warp and woof?'

'On the worlds of the stars, O Gārgī.'

'On what then, pray, are the worlds of the stars woven, warp and woof?'

'On the worlds of the Gods, O Gārgī.'

'On what then, pray, are the worlds of the Gods woven, warp and woof?'

'On the worlds of Indra, O Gārgī.'

'On what then, pray, are the worlds of Indra woven, warp and woof?'

'On the worlds of Prajāpati, O Gārgī.'

'On what then, pray, are the worlds of Prajāpati woven, warp and woof?'

'On the worlds of Brahma, O Gārgī.'

'On what then, pray, are the worlds of Brahma woven, warp and woof?'

Yājñavalkya said: 'Gārgī, do not question too much, lest your head fall off. In truth, you are questioning too much about a divinity about which further questions cannot be asked. Gārgī, do not over-question.'

Thereupon Gārgī Vācaknavī held her peace.[20]

The internal route took the form of the search for the ultimate ground of one's being or personality.

> But what *was* the essential self of man? The term introduced into Vedic inquiry was the common word for "self," *ātman*, used generally as a reflexive pronoun. From this general usage, *ātman* was given a more specific meaning as the essential part of man, his basic reality. At times this was taken to be the body or the trunk of the body as distinguished from the limbs. Gradually, however, the *ātman* was distinguished from the gross physical body; it was the *inner* self, the principle or entity that gave man his essential nature.[21]

The following Upaniṣadic passage (*Bṛhadāraṇyaka Upaniṣad IV. 1-6*) also provides a useful scriptural if simple illustration of this kind of an internal approach.

The light of man is the soul

1. Yājñavalkya came to Janaka, [king] of Videha. He thought to himself: *I will not talk.*

   But [once] when Janaka, [king] of Videha, and Yājñavalkya were discussing together at an Agnihotra, Yājñavalkya granted the former a boon. He chose asking whatever question he wished. He granted it to him. So [now] the king, [speaking] first, asked him"

2. *Yājñavalkya, what light does a person here have?*

   He has the light of the sun, O king, he said, 'for with the sun, indeed, as in his light one sits, moves around, does his work, and returns.'

'Quite so, Yājñavalkya.

3. 'But when the sun has set, Yājñavalkya, what light does a person here have?'

'The moon, indeed, is his light,' said he, 'for the moon, indeed, as in his light one sits, moves around, does his work, and returns.'

'Quite so, Yājñavalkya.

4. 'But when the sun has set, and the moon has set, what light does a person here have?'

'Fire, indeed, is his light,' said he, 'for with fire, indeed, as in his light one sits, moves around, does his work, and returns.'

'Quite so, Yājñavalkya.

5. But when the sun has set, Yājñavalkya, and the moon has set, and the fire has gone out, what light does a person here have?'

'Speech, indeed, is his light,' said he, 'for with speech, indeed, as in his light one sits, moves around, does his work, and returns. Therefore, verily O king, where one does not discern even his own hands, when a voice is raised, then one goes straight towards it.'

'Quite so, Yājñavalkya.

6. But when the sun has set, Yājñavalkya, and the moon has set, and the fire has gone out, and speech is hushed, what light does a person here have?'

'The soul (*ātman*), indeed, is his light,' said he, 'for with the soul, indeed, as in his light one sits, moves around, does his work, and returns.[22]

Elsewhere in the Upaniṣads a more detailed analysis of the human personality is carried out in an attempt to identify the *ātman*. One such analysis is characterised by its division of the human person into five sheaths, while another focuses on the states of consciousness experienced by the human being.

The *Taittirīya Upaniṣad* (2. 1-6) speaks of the five sheaths or *kośas*, which the human personality may be said to consist of. "In this passage an attempt is made to analyze man at five levels—proceeding from the grosser forms to the subtler, and, therefore, more real forms. The *real* man transcends the physical, vital, mental, and intellectual aspects and even the beatific aspect. It is in the end suggested that the real self of man is identical with Brahman, the ultimate principle, the absolute, which is its raison d'être'."[23]

Similarly, in another account (*Chāndogya Upaniṣad* 8: 7-12) "the real essential self is successively identified with the bodily self, the dream self, and the self in deep sleep, and it is suggested that all these three teachings are quite inadequate, for none of the three conditions, namely, of wakefulness, of dream and of deep sleep, can the nature of the self be said to conform."[24] The point is pressed that "the real self is neither body, mind nor complete negation of consciousness. The self is certainly conscious but of nothing else but itself. It is pure self consciousness as such and it is in this condition that it is identical with the highest reality."[25] This picture is fully elaborated in the *Māṇḍūkya Upaniṣad.*[26]

State of Consciousness	State of Self
Waking	Vaiśvānara
Dreaming	Taijasa
Deep Sleep	Prājña
The Fourth	Ātman

In the foregoing passages one notices how, as a result of going *inward* within the human personality, the Upaniṣadic seers identified the *Ātman*, as the real self, whether such an exercise focused on the constituents of the self (as in the case of the five sheaths) or on the states of consciousness experienced by the self (namely waking, dreaming and deep sleep). One needs to remind oneself now that as a result of going *outward* into the universe, the Upaniṣadic seers identified its real basis as *Brahman*, while looking inward the

Upaniṣadic thinker realised the inner self to be *Ātman*.[27]

Now the great discovery the Upaniṣads made was of the identity of the ground of the universe with the ground of our own being. Ainslie Embree elaborates this point with the help of three passages cited below. In the first he describes the quest of the ultimate ground of the objective universe, in the second of the individual subject. The two are brought together in the final passage.

> 1) In their quest for some ultimate ground for the world of natural phenomena, of time and space, and of human existence, the Upanishadic sages came to the conception of *brahman*, an undeniable, impersonal, unknowable power.[28]
>
> 2) Over against the questions concerning the ground of the external world are to be set those that probe inward, asking what is meant by the concept of the Self. The Self could be identified with the physical body, or "food," as some of the Upanishadic thinkers were inclined to say. But consciousness, breath, will, all had claims to be regarded as the Self, and all were unsatisfactory as final definitions. What was needed was something that could be identified as being beyond change, something that was in fact immortal. This was found in the conception of the *ātman*.[29]
>
> 3) In the macrocosm of the universe, the sages saw *brahman*; in the microcosm of their own being they saw the *ātman*. The realization that there is no distinction between the two, that the ground of one's own being is identical with the ground of the universe, is the great discovery of the Upanishadic thinkers. "Whoever thus knows, *I am brahman*," declares the sage, "becomes this all. Even the gods have not the power to prevent him from becoming thus, for he thus becomes the self." It should be carefully noted that this is not

> described as merging with the divine or union between God and man or reaching a state of unity. It is rather a recognition that there is no "divine" as distinct from the individual, no being over against the self, no process of becoming what once was not, but only the knowledge of the truth that always existed.[30]

This identification of *ātman* and *brahman* may be said to strengthen both, as it were. M. Hiriyanna points out, for instance, that the approach to the ultimate reality via Brahman runs into some difficulties:

> Such a principle need not be spiritual in its nature, and may well be a material or physical entity. Further, an objective conception like the above is little more than a hypothesis to account for the origin of the universe; and as there is nothing compelling us to regard it as actually existing, there being no logical absurdity in denying it. Some thinkers already seem to have done so in the Upanishadic period and maintained that 'in the beginning this world was just non-being.'[31]

Similarly, the approach to the ultimate reality via *ātman* is also not free from difficulties:

> If we start from the idea of the self, instead of that of Brahman, we meet with a similar difficulty, for, while the self points to what is spiritual and is an incontrovertible certainty, it is, as known to us, necessarily limited in its nature. Whatever view we may take of its nature, it is determined on one side by the world of nature, and on the other by the other selves.[32]

But when the two are identified they seem to have the effect of helping overcome each others' shortcomings. It was pointed out that Brahman as such might appear too hypothetical to be real. But by "its identification with *ātman* the establishment of the spiritual character of this principle and the removal of the uncertainty about its existence are both accomplished."[33] Similarly, it was hinted that the *ātman* may appear too personal, to the point of being limited, and finite, if very real; "it is this deficiency of finiteness that is made good by its identification with Brahman or the all-comprehensive first cause of the universe."[34]

This identification of *ātman* and *brahman* is capable of being interpreted in several ways. Troy Wilson Organ notes some of these in the following passage:

> The question to be asked first is about the meaning of the connective "is." The word "is" has at least five logically discernible meanings: 1) predication, e.g., "This apple is green"; 2) class inclusion, e.g., "Fido is a dog"; 3) class membership, e.g., "Brown pelicans are vanishing"; 4) equality, e.g., "Two and two is four"; 5) identity, e.g., "IV is [equivalent to] 4." *Ātman* is Brahman seems to be a form of identity or equivalence. There are many classes of identity: 1) absolute physical identity, e.g., "A is identical with A"; 2) relative physical identity, e.g., identical twins; 3) same entity at various stages of development, e.g., Joe Doakes as boy and J.D. as man; 4) same species, e.g., Harry Truman as man and Herbert Hoover as man; 5) same being in different contexts, e.g., Jane as mother and Jane as wife; 6) whole and part, e.g., a cup of water dipped from the Atlantic Ocean and the Atlantic Ocean; 7) appearance and reality, e.g., a photograph and the person of whom it is a photograph; 8) the same object considered from different perspectives, e.g., the duck-rabbit example of perception. Probably the last subclass of identity is the identity of *Ātman* and Brahman: *Ātman* is Totality viewed internally; Brahman is Totality viewed externally.[35]

The main point to note here is that the identity must be

understood ontologically. The passage cited above helps explain what is meant by identity. It is equally important to realize what is *not* meant by identity. First, when it is claimed in Advaita Vedānta that Ātman is Brahman, it is not claimed that Ātman *becomes* Brahman, as, for example, in a moment of realization. If anything, the realization consists of the fact that Ātman is Brahman, was Brahman, and will ever be Brahman. The point may be explained with the help of the parable "Like the King's Son," in which "a prince, brought up as a hunter from infancy, discover[s] afterward that he is of royal blood. It involves no becoming, for he has always been a prince and that all he has to do is to feel or realize that he is one."[36] The metaphysical moral of the whole story is that there was never a time when the mountaineer was not the Prince. He did not become a Prince when told he was one. He already was. He only recognized as a fact something that was already true.

Second, when it is claimed in Advaita Vedānta that Ātman is Brahman it is *not* meant that Ātman merges into Brahman. An example from astronomy will be helpful here. For a long time astronomers identified two distant stars—a "morning star" and an "evening star," till it was discovered that both were Venus. Did it then mean that the morning star merged into the evening star, or the evening star merged into the morning star? As both were already and always Venus, nothing of this sort can be said to have happened.

Third, it is sometimes suggested that " *Ātman is Brahman* is not a metaphysical statement but a soteriological statement."[37] Consider the following interpretation offered by Rudolph Otto: "The word *is* in the mystical formula of identification [Ātman is Brahman] has a significance which it does not contain in logic. It is no copula as in the sentence: s is P; it is no sign of equality in a reversible equation. It is not the *is* of a normal assertion of identity." In order to suggest what the statement is attempting to express, Otto adds, "For instance one might say instead of *I am Brahman, I am "existed" by Brahman* or *essenced* by Brahman, or *Brahman exists me.*" [38]The suggestion is intriguing but not acceptable as such within Advaita Vedānta.

Fourth, Ātman is Brahman does not mean that Ātman is a portion of Brahman. The *jīva* as the embodied Ātman may, in an extended sense, be said to be comprised in Brahman as parts of the universe of which it is the substratum but that is as much as one can say, for the truth of the matter is that "just as a pure transparent white crystal is wrongly imagined to be red on account of a red flower placed near it, or just as the colorless sky is wrongly imagined to be sullied with dirt by the ignorant, or just as the rope is wrongly taken to the be a snake in the twilight, or just as the shell is mistaken for silver, similarly the non-dual Ātman and Brahman is wrongly imagined to be the empirical self."[39] Śaṅkara's comment on *Brahmasūtra* 2.3.50 must be employed here to point out that "the individual soul is not directly the highest Ātman... nor is it different from Ātman." It is not the former because it is subject to the limiting adjuncts, but it is not different for it is also bereft of the limiting adjuncts. All the empirical selves are also comprised in Brahman, but the exact nature of their relationship is a matter of debate.[40]

That Thou Art

The fourth *mahāvākya* is: *That Thou Art.* An analysis of how this *great utterance* is to be understood provides a useful entry into the hermeneutics of Vedic statements.

It was pointed out earlier that, as distinguished from the other four orthodox schools of Hindu philosophy, those of Mīmāṁsā and Vedānta actually base their philosophy on the text of the Vedas rather than merely accepting Vedic authority as such in common with these other schools. It is therefore in these two schools that the issue of Vedic exegesis is squarely addressed. The key exegetical question as always is: how is the purport of a textual passage to be determined?

The Mīmāṁsā school of thought reached the conclusion that the purport of a textual passage should be determined by keeping six factors in mind. This six-fold criteria is technically called the *ṣaḍliṅga* and is said to consist of the following six elements:

> 1) unity of the initial and concluding passages (*upakramopasaṁhāraikya*); 2) the recurrence of theme (*abhyāsa*); 3) the new conclusion sought to be brought out (*apūrva*); 4) the fruitfulness of such a conclusion (*phala*); 5) the commendation or criticism of it throughout (*arthavāda*); 6) the argument throughout (*upapatti*). The Advaita Vedānta also accepts these criteria as the *pramāṇas* for finding *purport*.[41]

However, although both Mīmāṁsā and Advaita Vedānta accept these criteria, they assign interpretive priority to *different* parts of the Vedas—namely, the earlier sections and the latter sections respectively, and this accounts for the fact that they arrive at different conclusions regarding the purport of the Vedas while applying the same criteria. It should not be forgotten, however, that other systems of Vedānta besides Advaita also accept these criteria yet reach different conclusions regarding even the purport of the meaning of the "latter portion" of the Vedas. These differences, nevertheless, are the result of differences in interpretation of the same Vedic texts, whereas the difference between Mīmāṁsā and Vedānta, and particularly Advaita Vedānta, arise from the application of the same exegetical criteria to different sets of Vedic texts.

One may now proceed to examine how Advaitic exegesis works by applying it to a particular scriptural passage. The passage selected here is a famous one, which occurs in the *Chāndogya Upaniṣad*. It is in the form of a dialogue between a father (Uddālaka) and his son (Śvetaketu). The following extract provides the setting:

1. Om! Now, there was Śvetaketu Āruṇeya. To him his father said: 'Live the life of a student of sacred knowledge. Verily, my dear, from our family there is no one unlearned [in the Vedas] (*an-ucya*), a Brahman by connection (*brahma-bandhu*), as it were.'

2. He then, having become a pupil at the age of twelve, having studied all the Vedas, returned at the age of twenty-four, conceited, thinking himself learned, proud.

3. Then his father said to him: 'Śvetaketu, my dear, since now you are conceited, think yourself learned, and are proud, did you also ask for that teaching whereby what has not been heard of becomes heard of, what has not been thought of becomes thought of, what has not been understood becomes understood?'

4. 'How, pray, sir, is that teaching?'

5. 'Just as, my dear, by one piece of clay everything made of clay may be known—the modification is merely a verbal distinction, a name; the reality is just "clay".

6. Just as, my dear, by one copper ornament everything made of copper may be known—the modification is merely a verbal distinction, a name; the reality is just "copper".

7. Just as, my dear, by one nail scissors everything made of iron may be known—the modification is merely a verbal distinction, a name; the reality is just "iron" so, my dear, is that teaching'.

8. 'Verily, those honored men did not know this; for, if they had known it, why would they not have told me? But do you, sir, tell me it.'

So be it, my dear,' said he.[42]

We plug into the ongoing discussion at a point when the father is explaining the spiritual import of death to his son:

> 9. On this point, my dear, understand that this (body) is a sprout which has sprung up. It will not be without a root.
>
> 10. Where else could its root be than in water? With water, my dear, as a sprout, look for heat as the root. With heat, my dear, as a sprout, look for Being as the root. All creatures here, my dear, have Being as their root, have Being as their abode, have Being as their support.
>
> But how, verily my dear, each of these three divinities, upon reaching man, becomes threefold, as has previously been said.
>
> When a person here is deceasing, my dear, his voice goes into his mind; his mind, into his breath; his breath, into heat; the heat, into the highest divinity.
>
> 11. That which is the finest essence— (7) the whole world has that is its soul. That is Realty (*satya*). That is Ātman (Soul). That art thou, *Śvetaketu.*

'Do you, sir, cause me to understand even more.'

'So be it, my dear,' said he.

The reader will notice that the *mahāvākya* under discussion: *That art thou* has made its appearance in this piece of dialogue between the father and the son. It will recur eight more times and the passages in which it forms the concluding statement are reproduced below. In these passages, however, the same *mahāvākya* appears in different contexts. I shall therefore introduce each occurrence with a brief note, indicating the point to look for. In the next occurrence, for instance, the *metaphor of honey* is used. It could be argued that, among other things, the passage highlights the bliss that flows from the realization of the identity of

Ātman and *Brahman,* symbolised by honey.[43]

1. 'As the bees, my dear, prepare honey by collecting the essences of different trees and reducing the essence to a unity,
2. as they are not able to discriminate "I am the essence of this tree," "I am the essence of that tree"—even so, indeed, my dear, all creatures here, though they reach Being, know not "We have reached Being."
3. Whatever they are in this world, whether tiger, or lion, or wolf, or boar, or worm, or fly, or gnat, or mosquito, that they become.
4. That which is the finest essence – this whole world has that as its soul. That is Reality. That is Ātman (Soul). That art thou, *Śvetaketu.*

'Do you, sir, cause me to understand even more.'

'So be it, my dear,' said he.

In the following passage the *metaphor of the ocean* is used. It has been proposed that the passage hints at the immensity of the experience of the ultimate reality. The loss of individuality, yet its persistence as universality is hinted at.[44] The river ceases to be the river, but does not thereby cease to be.

1. 'These rivers, my dear, flow, the eastern toward the east, the western toward the west. They go just from the ocean to the ocean. They become the ocean itself. As there they know not "I am this one," "I am that one"
2. Even so, indeed, my dear, all creatures here, though they have come forth from Being, know not "We have come forth from Being." Whatever they are in this world, whether tiger, or lion, or wolf, or boar, or worm, or fly, or gnat, or mosquito, that they become.
3. That which is the finest essence—this whole world has that as its soul. That is Reality. That is Ātman (Soul). That art thou, *Śvetaketu.*

'Do you, sir, cause me to understand even more.'
'So be it, my dear,' said he.

In the following passage the *metaphor of the tree* has been employed. It highlights the intrinsic immanence and interpenetration involved in the identification of *ātman* and *brahman.*

This passage is best understood perhaps in the light of the following comment by Heinrich Zimmer: "According to this Brahmanical formula, the dialectic of the universe is a manifestation of a transcendent, non-dual, trans-dual, yet immanent principle, which both gives forth the world of names and forms (*nāmarūpa*) and inhabits it as its animating principle. The dualism of *natura naturans (prakṛti)* and the transcendent immaterial monad (*puruṣa*) is thus itself transcended".[45]

1. 'Of this great tree, my dear, if some one should strike at the root, it would bleed but still live. If some one should strike at its middle, it would bleed, but still live. If some one should strike at its top, it would bleed, but still live. Being pervaded By Ātman (Soul), it continues to stand, eagerly drinking in moisture and rejoicing.
2. If the life leaves one branch of it, then it dries up. It leaves a second; then that dries up. It leaves a third; then that dries up. It leaves the whole; the whole dries up. Even so, indeed, my dear, understand,' said he.
3. 'Verily, indeed, when life has left it, this body dies. The life does not die.

That which is the finest essence—this whole world has that as its soul. That is Reality. That is Ātman (Soul). That art thou, *Śvetaketu.*

'Do you, sir, cause me to understand even more.'
'So be it, my dear,' said he.

In the following passage the 'metaphor of the seed' is

used. It highlights the subtlety of the identity of *Brahman* and *ātman*; among other things. J. Brereton summarizes its significance as follows:

> First, the passage establishes that the tree grows and lives because of an invisible essence. Then, in the refrain, it says that everything, the whole world, exists by means of such an essence. This essence is the truth, for it is lasting and real. It is the self, for everything exists with reference to it. Then and finally, Uddālaka personalizes the teaching. Śvetaketu should look upon himself *in the same way*. He, like the tree and the whole world, is pervaded by this essence, which is his final reality and his true self.[46]

There may also be the implication here that "the world which has name and form arises from pure being which is subtle and does not possess name and form."[47] The passage runs as follows:

1. 'Bring hither a fig from there.'
   'Here it is, sir.'
   'Divide it.'
   'It is divided, sir.'
   'What do you see there?'
   'These rather (*iva*) fine seeds, sir.'
   'Of these, please (*aṅga*), divide one.'
   'It is divided, sir.'
   'What do you see there?'
   'Nothing at all, sir.'
2. Then he said to him: 'Verily, my dear, that finest essence which you do not perceive—verily, my dear, from that finest essence this great Nyagrodha (sacred fig) tree thus arises.
3. Believe me, my dear,' said he, 'that soul which is the finest essence – this whole world has that as its soul. That is Reality. That is Ātman (Soul). That art thou, *Śvetaketu*.

'Do you, sir, cause me to understand even more.'
'So be it, my dear,' said he.

The following passage may be read as an answer to the question: if Pure Being is the essence of all that exists, why is it not perceived?" The answer proposed is through the *parable of the salt*. Just as "we are able to perceive salt in the water [through taste] though not by means of touch and sight even so we will be able to perceive Pure Being by other means though it is not obvious to our senses".[48] The passage hints at the transcendental yet experienceable nature of the identity of *ātman* and *Brahman*.

1. 'Place this salt in water. In the morning come unto me.'
   Then he did so.
   Then he said to him: 'That salt you placed in the water last evening—please bring it hither.'
   Then he grasped for it, but did not find it, as it was completely dissolved.
2. 'Please take a sip of it from this end,' said he. 'How is it?'
   'Salt.'
   'Take a sip from the middle,' said he. 'How is it?'
   'Salt.'
   'Take a sip from that end,' said he. 'How is it?'
   'Salt.'
   'Set it aside. Then come unto me.'
   He did so, saying, 'It is always the same.'
   Then he said to him: 'Verily, indeed, my dear, you do not perceive Being here. Verily, indeed, it is here.
3. That which is the finest essence—this whole world has that as its soul. That is Reality. That is Ātman (Soul). That art thou, *Śvetaketu*.

'Do you, sir, cause me to understand even more.'
'So be it, my dear,' said he.
The next passage contains the *parable of the blindfolded*

person. Since at the moment we are blind to the reality, how might we reach it? This passage emphasizes the advisability of having a suitable guide or teacher. As Franklin Edgerton noted long ago:

> This section contains the beautiful simile of the man brought to a strange land and left blindfolded to wander about aimlessly, until some one removes his eye-bandage and tells him in which direction to go: then he finds his way home. Just so a man in this world who has not received the true instruction in Upaniṣadic philosophy wanders about aimlessly, his mental eyesight dimmed by the eye-bandages of ignorance, until a teacher removes the bandage of ignorance and tells him in what direction to shape his life's course; then he will arrive at his true goal.[49]

1. 'Just as, my dear, one might lead away from the Gandhāras a person with his eyes bandaged, and then abandon him in an uninhabited place; as there he might be blown forth either to the east, to the north, or to the south, since he has been led off with his eyes bandaged and deserted with his eyes bandaged;
2. as, if one released his bandages and told him, "In that direction would be the Gandhāras; go in that direction!" he would, if he were a sensible man, by asking [his way] from village to village, and being informed, arrive home at the Gandhāras—even so here on earth one who has a teacher knows: "I shall remain here only so long as I shall not be released [from the bonds of ignorance.] Then I shall arrive home."
3. That which is the finest essence—this whole world has that as its soul. That is Reality. That is Ātman (Soul). That art thou, *Śvetaketu.*

'Do you, sir, cause me to understand even more.'

'So be it, my dear,' said he.

In the following passage the significance of this insight in the context of the *experience of death* is explained. The implication seems to be that in dying a person, who has realized the identity of *Ātman* and *Brahman*, transcends all forms of phenomenal existence in a post-mortem state.

1. 'Also, my dear, around a [deathly] sick person his kinsmen gather, and ask, "Do you know me?" So long as his voice does not go into his mind, his mind into his breath, his breath into heat, the heat into the highest divinity—so long he knows.
2. Then when his voice goes into his mind, his mind into his breath, his breath into heat, the heat into the highest divinity—then he knows not.
3. That which is the finest essence—this whole world has that as its soul. That is Reality. That is Ātman (Soul). That art thou, *Śvetaketu.*

'Do you, sir, cause me to understand even more.'
'So be it, my dear,' said he.

In the following passage 'the metaphor of the heated axe of the ordeal' is proposed. It highlights the invulnerability conferred by the realization of the identity, through what to some might seem a measure of overconfidence in the ability of metaphysical reality to affect empirical reality.[50]

1. 'And also, my dear, they lead up a man seized by the hand, and call: "He has stolen! He has committed a theft! Heat the axe for him!" If he is the doer thereof, thereupon he makes himself (*ātmānam*) untrue. Speaking untruth, covering himself with untruth, he seizes hold of the heated axe and is burned. Then he is slain.
2. But if he is not the doer thereof, thereupon he makes himself true. Speaking truth, covering himself with truth, he seizes hold of the heated axe and is not burned. Then he is released.
3. As in this case he would not be burned [because of the truth]. So this whole world has that [truth] as its soul. That is Reality. That is ātman (Soul). That art thou, *Śvetaketu.*

Then he understood it from him—yea, he understood.[51]

Let us now apply the six-fold criteria to determine the import of the culled passages. The *first* criterion pertains to the unity of the initial and concluding passages. The initial passage states: "That Art Thou", and so does the concluding passage. The *second* criterion consists of thematic repetition. The statement "That Art Thou" is repeated "nine times"[52] in the selection. The *third* criterion consists of novelty. The claim "That Art Thou" is novel to the point of being sensational. The *fourth* criterion pertains to the result. The acquisition of knowledge, even saving knowledge, is the result. The *fifth* criterion is commendation. Quite obviously this insight is commended throughout, and the fact of it being dealt with throughout also fulfils the *sixth* and final criterion. Note that the purport is that of the non-duality between "That" and "This."

Now that the purport has been established, how is it to be understood – literally or figuratively?[53]

Śaṅkara takes it primarily in a literal sense,[54] and the point is made strongly in Advaita Vedānta that the "sentence expresses apposition (*samānādhikaraṇa*) between the two, Brahman and the individual soul."[55]

From the point of view of Advaita Vedānta the fact that the two are in apposition is important, because it enables one to point out that how the statement may not be (mis-) understood. (1) It is not to be understood as a tautology because "the Upaniṣadic sentence removes the delusion of difference between Brahman and the individual soul, even though their identity is known as soon as the true nature of both is known. For, Brahman is the self of all, and the 'Self' is not really the body or the ego, but Being."[56] 2) It is not to be understood as an identity between two *different* things as cause and effect ("The pot *is* earthen") or substance and attribute ("The lotus *is* blue") because here the identity of a thing with itself is asserted. 3) It is not to be understood as an injunction to treat them as such, as for instance in meditation, because the sentence has no reference to action. It is a statement of fact, not an exhortation.[57] 4) It is not to be understood as implication. This view "is based on the presupposition that words refer directly to substantives and not to attributes of substantives, and that when words have to refer to attributes they do so by implication."[58]

> A critic may ask, 'If it is said that here the identity of the substantives only—Brahman and jīva—is asserted, how have been they distinguished from their attributes?' An Advaitin may answer that other Hindu schools (e.g. that of Rāmānuja) also accept omniscience etc., as attributes of Brahman and ignorance etc., as attributes of jīva. Further, as will be shown later, prior to the hearing of *That Thou art* the meanings of *Thou* and *That* should be *clarified* (*tattvam-padārtha-śodhanā*). When a man, who has *clarified* for himself the meanings of these words, hears the sentence *That Thou art,* he will obviously understand that the asserted identity is only between the substantives and not between the attributes; just as when somebody tells him *bring the jar,* he understands by *jar* not *jarhood,* but a particular thing. If, then, the question occurs to him, *what happens to the attributes?* scriptural texts, supplemented by reasoning, will demonstrate to him that they are products of māyā. Thus an Advaitin can try to rebut this criticism.[59]

Brahman is Spirit

One may now examine the fifth *mahāvākya,* that Brahman is spirit, i.e., that it is spiritual rather than material in nature.

In order to fully appreciate this *mahāvākya,* three realizations need to be made available to our consciousness. The first is that both material objects and immaterial conspicuousness are equally the components of everyday existence. This fact is so obvious that it runs the risk of being overlooked. Each individual is fully aware of material objects, as well as of the immaterial consciousness which characterizes the person as an individual subject. In fact every individual himself or herself possesses a body and a mind—one material, the other immaterial in nature.

The second point to recognize is that, as pointed out earlier, this pervasive fact gives rise to three fundamental philosophical positions. Although both matter and immaterial consciousness are equally given in human existence, one could argue that each could be an epiphenomenon of the other. In other words, although both are experienced as empirical reality, only one of the two—matter or spirit may constitute the ultimate reality. Thus one could argue for materialism on the ground that, in the last analysis, consciousness is a byproduct of material forces and processes. Just as wetness is a quality possessed by none of the two gases which compose water, consciousness could emerge as a property out of material bases. It could also be argued, from the other end of the spectrum, that consciousness is the only ultimate reality, and that matter is its product. Consciousness could produce matter just as the living body produces lifeless nails or hair. A third position, which refuses to reduce each to either is also possible —and may be described as that of fundamental dualism. It was noted earlier that the various schools of Indian Philosophy can be arranged on an axis of:

Materialism..... Dualism..... Idealism.....

In the usual order of enumeration of these systems one starts with the Cārvāka school, regularly characterized as materialists, and one concludes with the discussion of schools of Vedānta which are prevailingly idealistic. This also holds true of Advaita Vedānta even more so.

A third point now requires to be considered: that it is difficult to refute the claims of materialism or idealism on *purely* logical grounds.[60] In other words, we seem to run here into the limits of reason, so that the significance to be attached to scriptural authority in general, and Advaita Vedānta in particular, takes on a new charge.

With this in mind one may now approach the Advaitic position which aligns itself clearly with the ultimate reality of the spirit. The following passage provides a remarkably clear statement of the Advaitic position on this point:

> The Advaita definitely denies that there can be any relation at all between two such disparate entities as spirit and matter. But at the same time, it cannot be forgotten that our investigation of experience leads us to the conclusion that they are not only together but are often identified with each other as implied, for example, when a person says "I am walking." Here the act of walking is obviously a feature characterizing the physical body; and yet it is predicated of the person's self which is spiritual. The only explanation conceivable is that their association must be a mere appearance or, in other words, that the relation between them is ultimately false. Śaṁkara treats of this point in his celebrated preamble to the commentary on the Vedānta Sūtra, which is very brief and is written in what may be described as his "shorthand style." "The self or the *I-element*," he says there, "is so opposed to the not-self or the *Thou-element* that they can never be predicated of each other." A necessary corollary to this conclusion is that one of the relata is unreal. Both, of course, cannot be regarded as unreal, for in that case, since all the three elements—the two relata and the relation—become false, and since the idea of falsehood necessarily points to a standard of truth, we shall have to postulate another reality from the viewpoint of which we declare them to be false.

> The advaitin therefore takes for granted that it is matter which is false. The other alternative would result in materialism, whose untenability we have already seen.[61]

Advaita as pointed out in the passage, also argues against materialism. As M. Hiriyanna notes:

> But even at its best the materialistic theory carries no conviction with it, since it tries to account for the higher principle of mind by the lower one of matter. Starting with the existence of matter, it explains mind as only a function of it. But in thus starting, the theory has already taken for granted that there is no mind, although it is as much an implication of experience as matter. In fact, we have no conception at all of matter, except as it appears to an observing mind. Believing in the existence of the one thus amounts to believing in the existence of the other. The truth that may underlie the theory is that all the things of the world can finally be brought under a single head, but it is wrong to conclude from this that that unitary source is necessarily physical.[62]

The statement is not just negative. It can also be argued that the spiritual premise about the ultimate reality as *Brahman* is implied in its description as *saccidānanda.* Thus, M. Hiriyanna writes:

> The spiritual and unitary character of this absolute reality is very well expressed by the classical phrase *saccidānanda.* As a single term defining its nature, it is met with only in the later Upanishads; but its three elements—*sat, cit* and *ānanda*—are used of Brahman, singly and in pairs, even in the earliest of them. *Sat,* which means "being," points to the positive character of Brahman distinguishing it from all non-being. But positive entities, to judge from our experience, may be spiritual or not. The

next epithet *cit*, which means "sentience," shows that it is spiritual. The last epithet *ānanda*, which stands for "peace," indicates its unitary and all-embracing character, inasmuch as variety is the source of all trouble and restlessness. "Fear arises from the other," as a famous Upanishadic saying has it. Thus the three epithets together signify that Brahman is the sole spiritual reality of the Absolute, which comprehends not only all being (*sat*) but also all thought (*cit*) so that whatever partakes of the character of either must eventually be traced to it. In other words, it is the source of the whole universe, while it is self-existent and self-revealing, there being no other entity from which it could be derived or by which it might be made known.[63]

PART II

Advaita Vedānta: A Rational Approach

I

We may begin our rational analysis with any object found in the universe, even something as simple, as say, bracelet of silver, in order to illustrate the rational approach to Advaita Vedānta.

The examination of the bracelet might begin with the recognition of the fact that the bracelet is made of silver. It has its origin in silver, and as without silver the "bracelet of silver" would not exist, silver is the material cause of the bracelet. The "bracelet of silver", in this way of looking at it, is thus an effect, with silver as its *material* cause.

The next step would now consist of examining the relationship of this bracelet, as effect, to silver which is its material cause. When the relationship between the two is closely examined, some points seem to emerge in clearer view as a result of this inquiry. It turns out that the effect is nothing more than the cause—that is to say, the bracelet is made of nothing other than silver. Note that one is not claiming that the bracelet is nothing more than the silver, in the sense that it is silver cast in a particular form and can be worn on the wrist, in a way plain silver cannot be worn. In this sense the bracelet of silver could be taken to mean to be "more" than silver. However, one can make bracelets of different shapes and sizes out of the same piece of silver but even in the new forms the material of which the form is made is nothing other than silver. In this sense the effect does not exceed the cause; "the effect is nothing more than the cause."

Moreover, although we might draw a distinction, when we speak, between a "bracelet of silver" and silver, as it were, the two are really inseparable. Or to put it another way, just as an effect is nothing more than the material cause, it is also nothing less than it, in the sense that it cannot be removed or divorced from it. That is to say, the effect cannot exist without the cause; we can separate the *idea* of the bracelet from the bracelet, but we cannot separate the bracelet of silver from silver. The bracelet of silver is shot through with silver, through and through.

So the first realization is that the effect is nothing more than the material cause, and the second is that the effect is inseparable from the material cause. These points are more or less obvious but no less significant is a third point—that the effect must pre-exist in the material cause. The 'idea' of a bracelet can exist apart from the material cause, but the actual bracelet, as effect, must pre-exist in the material cause. If this were not the case,

> then it would in principle be possible to produce any effect from any material cause. In fact, we cannot even think of a non-[pre]-existent entity coming into existence. We can only think of a substance changing from one form into another. If something non-existent could ever be brought into existence, there would be no reason why we could not press oil out of sand (where it is non-existent), and why we should have to select only a particular material, namely oilseed, to produce the particular effect oil."[64]

It might be helpful to locate the discussion somewhat, at this stage, both in terms of Indian and Western philosophy. It should be clarified, in terms of Western philosophy, that the discussion is proceeding by way of material cause in terms of Aristotle's four-fold formulation of material, efficient, formal and final causes. From this perspective, for instance, "the activity of the efficient cause, the oilman, the potter or the goldsmith [or the silversmith in the case of the silver bracelet] cannot produce any new substance, it only manifests the form of the substance concealed in its previous state."[65]

In terms of Indian philosophy, the context is provided by the doctrines of Asatkāryavāda and Saṭkārayaṿāda. According to the former view the effect is something "new" and doesn't pre-exist in the material cause. According to the latter the effect pre-exists in the material cause. It should be obvious from the trend of the arguments made earlier that Advaita Vedānta inclines towards the second view.

Hindu thinking further diverges in relation to the latter view on the point as to whether such effect represents an actual or apparent transformation of the material cause. According to the Sāṅkhya school, the effect represents an actual transformation of the material cause, as when a piece of silver is transformed into bracelet of silver, which it was not before.

The Advaitin joins issue with the Sāṅkhya school here because to claim that silver has been changed into a "new" form in the process implies that what was not has come into being—for that is what "new" must mean here; or the claim that silver has been transformed into what it was not earlier. From this point of view it can be said that according to Advaita, Sāṅkhya fails to realize the full significance of Satkāryavāda:

> For, it holds that though the effect exists previously in its material cause, there is real change (pariṇāma) of the material into the effect, since the material assumes a new form. Now this view amounts to the confession that this form, which did not exist previously, comes into existence. The doctrine of Satkārya-vāda, that nothing, which didn't exist previously, can come into existence, thus breaks down. If the grounds on which that doctrine stands are sound, then we must be prepared to accept all that logically follows from it, and cannot hold any view which implies any violation of this doctrine, rationally established.[66]

Some have even suggested that the Advaita doctrine should, by contrast, be called *Satkāraṇavāda*, because according to the Advaita doctrine that effects can never overreach or outreach the cause.

At stake here is the question : What is the logical, 'as distinguished from the perceptual', status of change of form ? Or, in other words, does change of form amount to change of reality ? The reality, which underlies all changes of forms, is the substance itself. Change of form doesn't amount to change of substance and if the substance remains the *same* through the *various* forms it assumes, can the changes be said to be real ? As there is no real change in this sense, can change be said to be real ? Thus :

> We have no reason, therefore, to interpret the perception of a change in form as a change of reality. On the contrary, it is found that in spite of changes in form a substance is recognized by us as the identical entity. Devadatta, sitting, standing or lying is recognized as the identical person. How can this be, if change in form implied change in reality?[67]

In this analysis the rational status of anything characterized by a quality, or any form characterized by change, is challenged. To go back to the silver bracelet. Thus the silver bracelet possesses this quality of having *curved.* Let us now pose the question: what is the relationship of the curve of the bracelet to the bracelet ? The curve does not consist of anything other than the bracelet itself, i.e.; it characterizes nothing else than the bracelet. Nor is the curve separable from it materially. Nor could the curve have come into being if it had not existed in the bracelet of silver as a potential. Thus the quality of the curvature of the silver bracelet has no existence apart from the silver bracelet.

Similarly, the silver bracelet has no existence apart from silver, as established earlier.

At the heart of the issue lies the question of the relationship of the quality to object (curvature to bracelet) or of object to substance (silver bracelet to silver). If the identity of effect to cause is rejected, although argued for by Advaita, then one is left with the following logical options: 1) that the effect is distinct from the cause; or that 2) the effect constitutes an identity-cum-difference with the cause.

Let us now examine these two options.

We begin by assuming that the effect is distinct from the cause. This means that there is one thing called cause and another called effect and the two are distinct. If the two are distinct, but the cause produces the effect, then they must be linked in some way; that is to say, there must be a third entity, which links these two entities. But if such be the case then

> We would fail to explain the relation between the quality and its substance. For, two distinct realities cannot be conceived to be related without the help of a third entity to connect them. Now, as soon as we think of this third entity (which must be distinct from the two terms it attempts to relate) we have to think of a fourth relating entity, and also a fifth, which would relate the third with each of the first two terms respectively. Similarly, these fourth and fifth entities would require other similar media for relating them to the terms they themselves want to relate, and so on. There would then be an infinite regress (anavasthā). We can thus never come to the end of our supposition and there will never be a complete explanation of the relation between the quality and its substance. In other words, the supposition of any distinction in reality between any quality and its substance would be logically indefensible. So a form cannot be treated as a distinct reality, and no change in form can be logically accepted as a real change, unless there is change in substance.[68]

Entity A Entity B

Entity C

Entity D

(Connecting A and C)

Entity E

(Connecting A to D)

Entity F
(Connecting A and E)

But perhaps treating them as two distinct entities involves ontological violence and the relationship is more properly conceived of as identity-in-difference. Thus both silver and silver-bracelet are after all identical as *silver*, but the silver-bracelet is also different in also being a *bracelet.* Advaitins claim that this is no more logically helpful in solving the issue of the relationship between silver-bracelet and silver, than treating the two as distinct, although on the face of it seems to resolve the problem. If two objects are related by identity-cum-difference then it must mean that in some respect they are identical and in some respect different. However "neither of them can *as* such be both identical with and different from the other. It would mean that M is both N and not-N and that N is similarly both M and not-M, which is a violation of the law of contradiction. When two things are distinct in fact, they cannot be the same."[69] In other words they do not constitute identity-in-difference directly. But as M. Hiriyanna points out further:

> Thus we may say that M and N possess one or more common feature which may be represented by a and, at the same time exhibit differences represented by x and y respectively. According to this explanation, what is identical is quite distinct

> from what is different; yet the entities, viz. M and N, by virtue of such features, it may be said, are identical with and, at the same thing different from each other. Such an explanation may seem to solve the difficulty, but the solution is only apparent, for it merely shifts the difficulty to another set of things. It assumes that M and N are characterized by a x and a y respectively, and the assumption leaves us where we were, for we cannot satisfactorily explain the relation between a thing and its so-called characteristics. Now the relation between M and a x, to take only one of the entities, cannot be identity, for then the distinction between a and x would vanish, both being identical with the same M; and with it also the relation of identity-in-difference between M and N. Nor can a and x be different from M, for then their character, whatever it may be, will cease to affect M, and therefore also its relation to N. So we are driven to think of identity-in-difference as the only possible relation between these. That is, in explaining the relation in question between M and N, we presuppose the same relation within each of them; and pursuing the inquiry further will only lead to an infinite process.[70]

To illustrate: Let us propose that the color of silver is the common property (a) shared by the silver bracelet and silver but the differences between them consist of (x) in the form of undetermined form of silver as a mere lump and (y) in the form of the special shape of the bracelet.

Now, in the case of silver (M), what is the relationship of silver to (a) its color and (x) its indeterminate shape? The difference between (a) color and (x) indeterminate shape would vanish, if both are identical with the same M (silver). Nor can (a) and (x) be different from M, for then they would have no connection with M. Hence this relationship too would have to be described as identity-cum-difference.

Thus:

M		N	
Silver		Silver-bracelet	
	Identity-cum-difference		
Color (a)	Indeterminate Shape (x)	Color (a)	Bracelet Shape (y)
Identity-cum-difference		Identity-cum-difference	

The characterization (of identity-cum-difference) *between* M and N merely *shifts* within them, and so down the pike.

Thus, no logically satisfactory resolution in terms of other logical options seems possible. Nevertheless, the change is perceived, although it is rationally unexplained and, therefore, logically unacceptable. Hence the need to characterize it as appearance. The point may be elaborated as follows:

> ...we have seen that no causation involves any change in substance. Hence causation does not imply any real change. Moreover, as every change is a process of causation; there cannot be any change in reality. This amounts to the position that though we perceive changes we cannot rationally accept them as real. We have therefore to understand them in the same way as we do, when we perceive an illusory object. We do perceive a rainbow, a blue sky, movement of the sun and many other things which we cannot believe as real because reasoning proves them to be unreal. Such a perceived but unreal phenomenon is called an appearance and distinguished from reality. On the same ground we must call change also an appearance and distinguish it from reality. We can thus reach, on purely logical grounds supported by common observation, the theory of vivarta or apparent change, as a rational doctrine required for the explanation of the world.[71]

One might be tempted to argue here in rebuttal, in terms of practical rather than pure reason, that the silver-bracelet is surely different from plain silver in that it can be worn on the wrist in a way one cannot wear plain silver. The Advaitin would counter argue that the fact that the bracelet is serviceable doesn't affect the truth of the proposition, no more than the apparent movement of the sun across the sky can be accepted as real just because it is helpful in organizing our daily activities. It is of service too but that doesn't make it true.

II

So we started with the examination of the relationship of the curve of the silver bracelet to the silver bracelet, preceded to an examination of the relationship of silver-bracelet to silver and found that the new relationship reincarnates the old problem. One might, however, at this point raise the following objection—what you say seems to hold for the objects in the universe, but does this also hold for the universe itself treated as an object, as it were. In other words, does what holds for the parts also hold for the whole?

Even this objection can be logically nuanced as follows: why speak of the universe, you speak of forms and substance but does what you say of forms apply to the substance also?

Both of these issues may now be dealt with in this section.

One must begin by recognizing that silver was chosen as a substance because, in relation to it, bracelets and other ornaments could be viewed as its modifications *(vikāra)* into form.

From a broader perspective, however, even silver is subject to modification *(vikāra)*. That is, it too is the form of some other substance X. Just as the bracelet arose out of silver, was in silver in some way before it so arose and dissolved into it again, so also silver itself is apparently the form of some substance X in which it pre-exists, from which it arises as silver and into which it disappears. Or to ring a metaphorical change, and talk of a pot of clay rather than a bracelet of silver:

> The qualities of a pot have no reality apart from the pot, and also that the pot itself has no reality apart from its cause, the clay, which is the real substance of which the pot is only one form of manifestation. But as clay itself is liable to modification and may cease to be clay, even it cannot be called a real substance; it is only a form of manifestation, though more abiding than a pot, of some other substance which persists through all the modifications of clay, and is also present in what clay itself comes from and in what it is changed into, after its destruction. If all so-called substances are thus liable to modification *(vikāra)*, then the substance underlying all objects of the world would be that which persists through all forms of objects. Existence is revealed in the perception of every object, whatever be its nature. It can, therefore, be called the substance, the material cause, or the underlying reality behind the world of objects.[72]

And now when we move to the level of the universe we do see a shift and a change in quantity does lead to change in quality in a quirky Marxian manner:

> If all so-called substances are liable to modification *vikāra* then the substance underlying all the objects of the world would be that which persists through all forms of objects. And we observe that existence (not in any specific form but existence pure and simple) is what is common to all forms of objects. Existence is revealed in the perception of every object, whatever be its nature. It can, therefore, be called the substance, the material cause of the underlying reality behind the world of objects.[73]

The qualitative change in the general conclusion should not go unnoticed. The attempt to analyze the nature of specific objects in the universe has led to the identification of non-specific existence as the material cause. The material cause has turned out to be immaterial existence! But this should not be considered unduly abstract. It is the neutral or unengaged gear in the car, which allows all specific gears to be engaged.

III

The next logical question to arise in the context is the following: this logical analysis pertains to the objective world. Does it also apply to the subjective world of the individual? Does Advaita Vedānta offer a different rational analysis for the internal world of being as opposed to the external?

This conclusion, that the material cause of the universe is immaterial existence, is also applied to the internal states in Advaita Vedānta, for these states also exist.

> ...when we examine the changing states within our minds what we also find there is that every state, every idea, whatever its object, exists. Even an illusory idea, which lacks an external object, exists as an idea (*avagati*). A state of deep dreamless sleep or of swoon also exists, although no objective consciousness is present there. Existence is thus found to be the one undeniable reality persisting through all states, internal and external. It can, therefore, be accepted as *the* substance, and material cause of which all determinate objects and mental states are the diverse manifestations.
>
> We find then that pure existence which is the common cause of the entire world is itself formless, though appearing in various forms; partless, though divisible in different forms; it is infinite though it appears in all finite forms. Śaṅkara thus reaches the conception of an infinite, indeterminate *nirviśeṣa* existence as the essence or material cause of the world. He calls this Absolute or Brahman.[74]

IV

This is how the rational investigation of everyday reality by Advaita leads it to question and then reconfigure the conceptual framework with *which* we operate in everyday life. In the course of ordinary living, we draw a sharp distinction between our experience of the external universe and our own inner life. Advaita Vedanta, however, pools our experiences of the external world and the internal world as data to be explained in common and is thus counter-intuitive in terms of our quotidian philosophical framework.

It questions this framework at an even deeper level, when it raises the question of the relationship of consciousness to existence. In terms of our quotidian or even commonsensical philosophy of life, we associate "existence" with our experience of the external world, and "consciousness" with our experience of the internal world. Thus for us external objects "exist" and we are "conscious" of our internal states.

In this context Advaitic rationality raises the question: What is the criterion of consciousness? Note the Advaitin answer to the parallel question: What is the criterion of existence? is the following: that which is perceived. The totally non-existent —the barren woman's son and the horns of a hare—cannot be perceived. Let a similar question now be posed in relation to consciousness.

> But what is the criterion of consciousness? A mental state is conscious, because its existence is self-revealing. But when we perceive the external world its existence also reveals itself. The power of appearing *bhāti* is common to both internal and external forms of existence; and it can, therefore, be argued that existence which is common to the internal and external world must posses the power of revealing itself. Therefore, it is more reasonable to hold that Absolute existence is of the nature of self-revealing consciousness. In fact, a little reflection shows that self-revelation may even be

> taken as the differential that distinguishes existence from non-existence. What is non-existent (e.g. the son of a barren woman) cannot even appear or reveal itself for a moment.[75]

The gulf we tend to sense between existence and consciousness is bridged in Advaita Vedānta by arguing that when we speak of the existence of the silver-bracelet it boils down to the consciousness of the existence of the silver-bracelet and that we would not be able to speak of the existence of silver apart from the consciousness of its existence.

In terms of another metaphor:

> Wherever there is appearance of existence there is awareness invariably present. Even an external object, say clay, which appears to us is presented by an awareness of clay (*mṛt-buddhi*). When we perceive clay becoming a pot, our clay-consciousness turns into pot-consciousness (*ghaṭa buddhi*). An imaginary object is just the idea of the object, and so also is an illusory object. So we find that awareness pervades all forms of existence known to us.
>
> By a series of arguments like these Śaṅkara reaches logically what he accepts on the authority of the revealed texts, namely that the world originates from Brahman, which is Absolute Existence and Consciousness and that Brahman has the power of manifesting itself in diverse apparent form, without really undergoing any modification.[76]

V

The tenor of our analysis of the world, however, has so far taken the smooth and easy route. We started out with the curve of the silver-bracelet, and moved through on to silver and to that substance of which the silver might only be one form, and ended up by identifying general existence as the material cause of the universe.

But the course of the universe is not that smooth. For one thing we find one experience of existence contradicted by another. What we thought was a snake turns out to be a rope. Similarly, the universe doesn't consist of just silver-bracelets or silver. It contains many other objects. In other words, our analysis of the universe needs to be made more complex by incorporating two new features of our experience into it: (1) the contradictability of objects and 2) the immense variety of objects. The question we must now answer is : how do these twin considerations affect the logic of the arguments advanced so far ?

We argued earlier from form to substance in a seamless way—but forms can contradict or replace one another over time and they vary in space. What bearing then do these factors have on the logical outcome of our discussion?

When experiences contradict one another, then the contradicting form takes precedence over or is considered more real than the contradicted form. Thus normal waking state is considered more real than dream state and within waking state, as when a piece of shell is experienced as silver, the contradicting experience (here shell) is considered more real than the contradicted experience (here silver).

> But in spite of such contradictions among the different forms, existence or (consciousness) as such remains uncontradicted. When we disbelieve an illusory serpent we only deny that the existence there is of a form of a serpent, but we do not deny that there is some existence. Again, even when we deny a dream object, we don't deny that the experience or idea existed. And when we think of a time or place where nothing exists, we are thinking of the existence of at least that time or place. So existence, in some form or another, is as wide as thought and we cannot conceive of the absence or denial of existence. This universal, pure existence (or consciousness) is thus the only thing

> whose contradiction is unthinkable. Śaṅkara calls it, therefore, supreme reality (*Pāramārthika sattā.*) He thus logically arrives also at his conception of reality as that which persists uncontradicted through all forms of existence in all place and times.[77]

But on what logical basis, we might wish to ask, was the *contradicting* experience considered superior to the *contradicted* experience? A little reflection leads to the conclusion that the contradicting experience is considered more real than the contradicted experience, because it endures longer than the contradicted experience. Thus waking state outlasts the dreaming state, and the experience of the rope lasts longer than that of the serpent.

This provides a clue to the Advaitic concept of reality namely, that that which persists is real. One is led in this direction by an examination of both the original argument and the complications introduced into it in this section. Thus, to revert to the original argument, the silver in a sense is more real since the bracelet was a form of it and the substance X, of which silver might be the form, is more real than silver because each respectively endures longer, and existence itself—pure indeterminate existence—was identified as the material cause of the universe because it was the most enduring of all.

This thrust is confirmed when one takes the fact that forms might contradict one another into account—as when the experience of a snake is contradicted by it turning out to a rope, or dream experience by waking experience. Existence as such persists through them also.

As for the diversity of objects exhibited by the universe, it needs to be noted that they are all undergoing modification, although at different rates. Even more important than the difference in the rate at which they are undergoing modification is the fact that they are all undergoing modification. Now

> This theoretical possibility of change in perception, and of consequent contradiction, then makes the

> status of every particular object precarious, in respect of its reality. We can never be absolutely certain that what appears now as pot will not appear otherwise later. We see, therefore, how different particular forms of existence, like pot and cloth, weaken and undermine each other's claim to indubitable reality. If, however, these claimed only pure existence, and not existence of particular forms, their claims would not have been mutually exclusive. The rival claims of particulars *as particular* existents thus prevent them from having the position of indubitable reality such as pure existence enjoys.[78]

VI

The upshot of such a rational analysis of the objective universe along Advaitic lines leads one to the following conclusion:

> On such rational grounds Śaṅkara grades and classifies common experience. As we saw, he first of all, distinguishes all objects of possible and actual experience from utter unreality, like the child of the barren mother. The former again are classed under there heads : 1) those that only appear momentarily in illusions and dreams, but are contradicted by waking experience, 2) those that appear in normal waking experience—the particular and changing objects, which form the basis of our ordinary life and practice, but which are still not acceptable to reason as completely real (because they exhibit contradiction or are open to future contradiction), and 3) pure existence which reveals itself through all experience, and is neither contradicted nor contradictable.[79]

How is such a world, the world not only of common experience, but one in which common experience is rationally described?

> The world is thus not a homogeneous conception, and if, in spite of this, one insists on being told what such a world, as a whole is, the fairest reply can only be, what Śaṅkara gives, namely that is indescribable (*anirvacanīya*) either as real or as unreal. But if the word world is confined only to the second aspect, it would be again fair to say, that the world is real only for practical purpose, more real than the first and less real than the third kind of existence. But if the world is taken in the third sense, Śaṅkara would emphatically assert that the world is eternally real. As he puts it : "As the cause, Brahman, doesn't lack existence at any time, past, present or future, so does the world not lack existence in any of the three periods of time." Again, " All particular modes of existence with different names and forms as real as existence, but unreal as particulars." [80]

VII

So much of the objective world—what now of the individual subject?

The rational analysis of the individual subject in Advaita seems to follow three routes: 1) an analysis of the subject's experience of itself; 2) an analysis of the subject's experience of the states in which it exists in the world and 3) and analysis of the subject in the light of its relation to the external world.

The subject's experience of itself is usually described through the use of the personal pronoun "I". One way in which Advaita arrives at its concept of the individual is through a rational analysis of this linguistic phenomenon.

The word "I" can be employed in various ways and if the common denominator underlying these various uses could be identified, then one might have here the key by turning which the secrets of the self may be unlocked. Some of such uses of the "I" may be listed as follows:

1. I am tall
2. I see you
3. I walk home
4. I think of it
5. I feel he is wrong
6. I will do it
7. I know, I just know

The first use refers to the body. So the "I" possesses a body. Thus people say: 'I am tall', 'I am short', 'I am fat;, 'I am thin' and so on.

The second use refers to an organ of perception—the eye. One also says: I hear, I touch, I taste, and I smell. Thus the organs of perception located in the body and their function are some of the things the "I" identifies with. It does the same when it says: I balance myself on a beam.

The third use refers to an organ of action, that of locomotion. One also says : I talk, I grasp, I empty my bladder, and I have sex. Thus the organs of action located in the body and their function are some of the other things the "I" identifies with.

The fourth, fifth, and sixth uses point to the psyche in its three dimensions of thinking, feeling and willing. The "I" identifies itself with each of these.

The seventh use points to the sense of intuition possessed by us—a sense of knowing somewhat different from our usual way of knowing things. The *I* identifies with it too.

Now what persists through all these states as a common denominator? One might be tempted to say the body, but the body could not identify with any of the descriptions offered earlier, were it not conscious. Neither would the mind be able to identify with any were it not conscious. In fact, the identification of the *I* with any of the descriptions offered earlier presuppose consciousness. Thus

> Consciousness is, therefore, the essence of the self in whichever form it may appear. But it is not consciousness of any particular form, but simple

> consciousness common to all its forms. Such consciousness is also pure existence since existence persists throughout all forms of consciousness. The different particular and changing forms of consciousness can be shown, from their contradictory natures, to be mere appearance, in the same way as the different forms of existence were shown to be so before. [81]

There are ostensibly moments, however, when consciousness is not present, as when we swoon or are asleep. At these moments, however, our sense of *I* also disappears. Thus the correlation between *I* and *I*-consciousness in terms of our *conscious* self is obvious. But what when we are dreaming? We are not conscious of our body when we are dreaming, although consciousness in some form is present. In deep sleep it seems to be absent at first sight.

This brings us to the second approach adopted in Advaita for identifying the nature of the self. All of us assert that I am awake, I dreamt, and I slept. Thus the *I* clearly persists through these three states of waking, dreaming and deep sleep. But does consciousness persist through these three states? According to Advaita an analysis of these three states reveals that consciousness does persist through them.

Moreover, as a bonus, this analysis also enables us to identify the nature of this consciousness more clearly, if we argue as follows:

> The essence of the self must remain in all these or the self would cease to be. But what do we find common to all these states ? In the first state there is consciousness of external objects; in the second also there is consciousness, but of internal objects present only to the dreamer. In the third state no objects appear, but here is no cessation of consciousness, for otherwise the subsequent memory of that state , as one of peace and freedom from worries, would not be possible. The persistent

> factor then is consciousness, but not necessarily of any object. This shows again that the essence of self is pure consciousness without necessary relation to objects. [82]

The identification of objectless consciousness through the rational analysis of deep sleep is very important from the point of view of Advaita. Normally, we always associate consciousness with an object but the phenomenon of deep sleep reveals that although consciousness need not always be associated with an object, it must always be associated with the subject.

The third approach to the individual subject identified in Advaita enables one to say more about the nature of pure consciousness. In this approach that fact that the individual subject stands face-to-face with a world of objects is subjected to radical rational scrutiny. The first result of such an investigation is the reconfiguration of the concept of subject and object as commonly understood in philosophy as follows:

> The cognitive situation is usually taken to involve a subject and object. The Advaitin substitutes for them *dṛk* and *dṛśya,* the former meaning the self or what reveals and the latter, what is revealed. The reason for this substitution is that the other division is not logically quite satisfactory. The subject includes not only *dṛk* but also *dṛśya.* It is really a complex of the self and the not self. This is clear from statements like *I know myself*;, where *myself* refers to some thought or feeling or, as Hume said, 'some particular perception or other, of heat or cold, light or shade, love or hatred, pain or pleasure.' These perceptions, being observable, are *dṛśya* and necessarily point to some center of consciousness beyond them. [83]

The *dṛk* or the individual subject, as the center of pure consciousness, upon analysis, displays certain striking properties.

> It is impossible to think of the absence of *dṛk*—as having ceased to be or as not having yet come to be, for that thought itself would imply the presence of *dṛk*. Hence *dṛk*, in some sense, should be regarded as having neither beginning nor end, and therefore as eternal or timeless.
>
> ...We have seen that *dṛk* cannot have internal parts. It cannot be externally related to other *dṛks*, for a similar reason, viz., that it is not possible to think of any dividing line between them. The only way in which we can distinguish between one *dṛk* and another is by reference to their content or the objects they reveal. In themselves, they are indistinguishable. That is, *dṛk* is one or, more strictly, not many.[84]

In this way the pure subject is not only external and *one*, it can also be considered all-comprehensive, if the *dṛśya* is considered dependent on the *dṛk* and therefore accounted for by *dṛk*, for then *dṛk* becomes "all-comprehensive, in the sense that there is nothing outside it", directly or indirectly.

VIII

The concept of contradiction plays a special role in logical analysis. We would do well, therefore, to analyze its role in Advaitic rationality.

In terms of pragmatic reason, Advaitic thinking would distinguish between contradiction between one thought and another, and between thought and practice. One could think of a situation, for instance, in which an individual is constantly changing his pattern of thought, so that what one says today may contradict what one said fifteen days ago. However, one might yet, in both these phases, be consistent in terms of thought and practice. Suppose, for instance, that fifteen days ago a person believed in violence *and also behaved violently*. Now, fifteen days later, the same person comes to believe in non-violence and *also behaves non-violently*. Then over this fifteen-day period he would have exhibited contradiction at the level of thought and also at the level of practice, but not at the level of the relationship between thought and practice. In terms of practical reason, as it were, one could display a pattern of four possibilities. 1) contradiction between thought and thought ; 2) contradiction between practice and practice; 3) thought contradicted by practice (when one thinks oneself to be detached and may not be) and 4) practice contradicted by thought (one may actually be modest and not think of oneself as such, as part of being modest!) . Then there is the case of the *jīvanmukta*, a case in which such contradictions might be considered unthinkable. This is then how the discussion of contradiction might well proceed in terms of Advaitic ethics and soteriology.

In the realm of Advaitic epistemology and ontology, however, the discussion of contradiction must be set on a different course. The referents of contradiction here are thought and experience. In terms of these referents one can again came up with a four-fold pattern; 1) the contradiction of one experience by another; 2) the contradiction of one thought by another; 3) the contradiction of thought by experience and 4) the contradiction of experience by thought.

An example of the contradiction of one experience by another is provided by the experience of what was thought to be snake turning out to be a rope. The experience of the rope contradicts the experience of the snake. Similarly, the experience of waking contradicts the experience of sleep. Note, however, that while in the first case the contradicting experience of the rope falsified the contradicted experience; this cannot be said of the contradiction involved in the waking and sleeping states. One can either accept both on their face value, or claim that each falsifies the other. This is possible because they belong to two different kinds of consciousness, unlike the case of the rope-snake example.

An example of the contradiction of one thought by another is provided when it is argued that the effect and (material) cause may be two distinct entities. This is contradicted by the thought that the two distinct entities require a third entity to relate them, but then this third entity will have to be related by a fourth and fifth entity to the first and so forth, leading to infinite regress.

The example of the contradiction of thought by experience will be provided by the case in which one might think it unthinkable that one could experience a state in which one is neither aware of oneself nor of the world. Yet the experience of dreamless sleep provides precisely an example of such a state, and so might *samādhi.*

The example of the contradiction of experience by thought is provided by the apparent movement of the sun across the sky. It is given by experience but contradicted by astronomical knowledge.

For the rational presentation of Advaitic ontology, however, this grid has to be ratched up a notch to another level: to the contradiction between the non-contradictable and the contradictable.

It was mentioned earlier how "universal, pure existence (or consciousness) is the only thing whose contradiction is unthinkable. Śaṅkara calls it, therefore, Supreme reality (*Pāramārthika Sattā*). He thus logically arrives also at this conception of reality as that which persists uncontradicted through all forms of existence in all places and times."[22] As distinguished from such existence in general, existence in the particular suffers from a liability. "About any definite or particular form of existence, which may appear in our experience, we can never be certain that it may not be supplanted by a contradictory experience arising in future. So the theoretical or logical possibility of it being contradicted is always there." [86]

The distinction between the contradiction of snake by rope; and of sleep by waking become relevant when it is claimed that *rationally* speaking, even two objects like pot *ghaṭa* and cloth *paṭa* falsify each other.

Rope and snake experienced in the same waking state as distinct objects do *not* falsify *each* other; when the *same* object which was perceived as a snake turns out to be a rope, one (snake) is falsified by the other (rope); waking and dreaming may be credibly said to falsify each other but they belong to two different orders of experience. It is true that both pot and cloth may be falsified, as particulars, in relation to universal existence but they can be said to *mutually* falsify each other only from the perspective of universal existence, as the uncontadictable reality in the light of which not only are both contradicted but also *mutually* so, even though they are at the same ontological level. In other works, change involves the possibility of contradiction, possible change therefore involves the possibility of contradiction but note that *experientially* the pot can never change into cloth because of acceptance of *satkāryavāda.* From the point of view of *satkāryavāda* both effects are false and doubly so but only mutually in relation to the highest level.

The paradox is that although logically the pot and cloth falsify each other on account of changeability, experientially they cannot change into *each* other. Logic from the highest level delimits experience of particulars, while logic at the same level limits experience to particulars. The rope can *apparently* turn into a snake but can the pot turn into cloth? No, but what they do is "weaken and undermine each other's claim to indubitable reality" by reinforcing each other's particularity.

PART III

Advaita Vedānta: An Experiential Approach

The experiential approach to the study of Advaita Vedānta provides a third possible way of approaching the subject. An initial validation for such an approach is provided by an attempt to answer the following question : Why should not a rational approach suffice either by itself, or in combination with the scriptural approach, to provide an introduction to Advaita Vedānta? Of course from a certain point of view it can. In fact, either the scriptural or the rational could suffice by itself for that matter. However, a more comprehensive perspective might lead one to conclude otherwise. Our experience of life reveals that life is characterized by three states of consciousness—waking, dreaming and deep sleep. A philosophy of life must take all three into account and account for all three. Rationality, however, is a characteristic of human mind only during the waking state, although mental activity in some form is common to both the waking state and the dreaming state. In the state of deep sleep, even mental activity, or at least conscious mental activity, also ceases. Thus rationality only characterizes a part of life, can it be used to account for the whole of life? The same argument can be given another form in terms of conscious mental activity, even during the waking state. Mental activity, in the waking state, also includes aesthetic and emotional experience. Thus rationality is only one, if privileged, aspect of this manifold mental activity. We give premium to rationality because we associate it with the philosophical enterprise in which we are engaged. Thus, its role gives it a certain status in view of the nature of the task we are engaged in but it is useful to be reminded of the fact that there is more to life than logic. What an electrifying insight this must have been before it became a cliché.

How then might Advaita Vedānta be presented, if it took all the states of existence and not just one (of which the experience of rationality is so striking a feature) into account?

II

One important feature of the experiential exposition of Advaita Vedānta is to question the finality of the distinction between waking and dreaming and deep sleep. In our everyday approach to life, if we were asked to pair out any two of them and separate the one left out as an indication in our judgement of their relative importance, then nine times out of ten we will be inclined to pair dreaming and deep sleep as one unit, and separate the waking state as the one in which we are really alive. The waking state lies at the center of our life. After all, we live from day-to-day, not night-to-night. The night is spent in repose and in experiencing the states of dreaming and deep sleep.

The Advaita approach to the matter, however, is more inclined to pair the states of waking and dreaming, and prefers to separate deep sleep from them for reasons which will now be explained. Advaita Vedānta is inclined to pair the waking and dreaming states together, notwithstanding their differences, because both of them are equally characterized by mental activity. According to the Advaitic view our concepts of space, time and causality differ in the waking and dreaming states, in contrast to the common view that these concepts are present in the waking state and absent in the dreaming state. According to Advaitins the only real difference between the two is duration—waking is a longer stretch of dreaming and that is why in the waking state we can recall we slept but not vice versa.

Many thinkers—both Eastern and Western—have felt that drawing a firm distinction between waking and dreaming presents difficulties. Among Western thinkers Descartes and Pascal may be specially mentioned. Descartes wrote:

> When I consider the matter carefully, I do not find a single characteristic by means of which I can certainly determine whether I am awake or whether I am dreaming. The vision of a dream and the experience of my waking state are so much alike that I am completely puzzled and I don't really know if I am not dreaming at this moment.[87]

And Pascal said :

> If a dream comes to us every night we should be as much occupied with it as by the thing we see every day, and if an artisan were certain that he would dream every night for twelve hours that he was a king, then he would be just as happy who dreams every night for twelve hours that he is an artisan.[88]

In the East, the Indian king Janaka and the Chinese philosopher Chuang Tzu were baffled, it seems, by similar experiences. There was once a famous Indian king called Janaka. "King Janaka had a dream that he was a beggar. On his waking up he asked his guru 'Am I a king dreaming of being a beggar or a beggar dreaming of being a king?"[89]

Chuang Tzu (c. 369-286 B.C), second in importance only to Lao Tzu as a representative of Taoism, raises for "epistemology... the ultimately unanswerable question":[90]

> Once upon a time, Chuang Chou [i.e. Chuang Tzu] dreamed that he was a butterfly, a butterfly fluttering about, enjoying it. It did not know that it was Chuang Chou again. But he didn't know whether he was Chuang Chou who had dreamed that he was a butterfly, or whether he was a butterfly dreaming that he was Chuang Chou. Between Chuang Chou and the butterfly there must he some distinction. This is what is called the transformation of things.[91]

In a less celebrated and more elaborate passage Chuang Tzu further considers the plausibility of the dream-like nature of life.

> Those who dream of a merry drinking party may the next morning wail and weep. Those who dream of wailing and weeping may in the morning go off gaily to hunt. While they dream they do not know that they are dreaming. In their dream, they may even try to interpret their dream. Only when they have awakened do they begin to know that they have dreamed. By and by comes a great awakening, and then we shall know that it has all been a great dream. Yet all the while the fools think that they are awake; this they are sure of. With minute nicety, they discriminate between princes and grooms. How stupid! Confucius and you are both in a dream. And when I say that you are in a dream, this is also a dream. This way of talking may be called paradoxical. If after ten thousand generations we could once meet a great sage who knew how to explain the paradox, it would be as though we met him after only one morning or one evening.[92]

A similar tendency to treat the waking state as analogous to dreaming also appears in Buddhist thought, as the following passage indicates:

> "The senses are as though illusions and their objects as dreams. For instance a sleeping man might dream that he had made love to a beautiful country girl, and he might remember her when he awoke. What do you think ...does the beautiful girl he dreamed of really exist?"
>
> "No, Lord."
>
> "And would the man be wise to remember the girl of his dreams, or to believe that he had really made love to her ?"
>
> "No, Lord, because she doesn't really exist at all, how could he have made love to her—though of

> course he might think he did under the influence of weakness or fatigue."
>
> "In just the same way a foolish and ignorant man of the world sees pleasant forms and believes in their existence. Hence he is pleased, and so he feels passion and acts accordingly[93]

Mystics even more than philosophers are inclined to disregard the distinction, at some level, between waking and dreaming, as in the following story narrated by Śrī Rāmakṛṣṇa Paramhaṁsa (1836-1886):

> A son was born to a king. He was the only child and was therefore *the apple of the eye* of both the king and queen. The prince became a favorite with all and as he grew older he was taught all the arts and the sciences. One day, all of a sudden, the prince fell ill. The malady went on getting worse and even the best physician of the kingdom found that all treatments were of no avail. Both the king and the queen never left his side day and night and the most competent physician and nurses continuously attended him. The king was exhausted by his constant vigil and one night he could not resist falling asleep. He was awakened by the sound of crying and weeping and learnt that prince had passed away while he was asleep. The king sat as if he was stupefied, without speaking a single word. The queen asked him how it was that on the passing away of the only a child whom he loved so much there was not a single drop of tears in his eyes. The king said, 'Oh queen, when I fell asleep I dreamt that I had become a monarch of a large kingdom, much larger than mine, and the father of seven worthy and ideal princes, each of whom was well trained in the art of administration. I handed over the charge of my kingdom to them and thereafter I was spending

> my days in peace and happiness with you. And now this tragedy has taken place and I am unable to make up my mind whether I should lament for the child that has left us today or whether I should mourn the loss of the seven sons and a vast kingdom: I see no difference in the two bereavements and to me the world has become nothing but a dream'.[94]

Ramaṇa Maharṣi (d. 1950) asserts even more directly the elusiveness of the distinction.

> All that we see is a dream, whether we see it in the dream state or waking state. On account of some arbitrary standards about the duration of the experience and so on, we call one experience a dream and another waking experience. With reference to reality both the experiences are unreal. A man might have such an experience as getting *anugrah* (grace) in his dream and the effects and influence of it on his entire subsequent life may be so profound and so abiding that one cannot call it unreal, while calling real some trifling incident in the waking life that just flits by is causal and of no moment and is soon forgotten. Once I had an experience, a vision or a dream whatever you may call it. I and some others including Chadwick who had a walk on the hill. Returning we were walking along a huge street with great buildings on either side. Showing the street and the buildings, I asked Chadwick and others whether anybody could say that what we were seeing was dream and they all replied, *What fool will say so ?* and we walked along and entered the hall and the vision or dream ceased, or [we] woke up. What are we to call this?[95]

A story told about the fifth Sikh Guru, Guru Arjun (1563-1606) also makes a similar point. It is said that a king came to visit him but

> when he heard the musicians hymning the Guru's composition saying "O friend, the Writ thy God has written out for thee can be obliterated not", he became anxious in the mind. On being questioned, the Guru explained to the visitor that the Writ that God writes is based upon one's own deeds. This gravely disappointed the King who asked:—"If such be the case what is the need of the Guru's Grace or even of doing or being good, if what has to happen must come to pass." The Guru replied:—"Of this we would talk tomorrow." In the night, the King dreamt that he had become a sweeper, clothed in tatters, dealing with filth all the time and living the life of a miserable wretch. He woke up, disturbed, in the morning and told the Guru so. The Guru replied: "O devotee, you slept as a King and in the dream became a poor wretch. Your dream-state was as valid at the time of your dreaming, as is your kingly state which you really possess. Such is the nature of the Guru's Grace that no matter what your past or present, you pass through, and are affected by it, only as one passes through a dream, till one's self awakens to realise the essential kingly nature of one's soul".[96]

The state of deep sleep presents a radical contrast to the states of waking and dreaming. The most striking features of this contrast are two-fold: (1) that in deep sleep one loses awareness of both oneself and of the world—outer as well as inner. In the waking state, one is aware of the world of external objects; in the dream state, one is aware of a world of external objects also (which upon waking are discovered to have been inner); but this crucial distinction disappears in deep sleep. (2)Although one thus undergoes loss of individuality in deep sleep yet upon waking one identifies oneself with the same person who went to sleep. This establishes that identity can survive loss of individuality. These two facts—that in deep sleep one loses all sense of individuality (as well as of the world) and further that despite this lapse in individuality one doesn't suffer loss of identity—are considered such sensational features of deep sleep that they—for the Advaitin—place deep sleep in a category by itself, in comparison with waking and dreaming taken together.

III

We revert now to the discussion of three states as separate ones, after noticing that the analysis of deep sleep leads us to the conclusion that there must be some entity which survives discontinuity as sharp as the one involved in the state of deep sleep, wherein even our sense of individuality is lost. We are now led to a larger question: what constitutes the underlying link even between the two different senses of individualities experienced by us in the waking and dreaming state respectively? Thus there is something which underlies and sustains both the changing individualities in waking and dreaming states, and the loss of individuality as such in the state of deep sleep.

One, thus, arrives at the concept of the pure subject, in the absence of which the three separate states couldn't possibly constitute the experience of a single person.

This is the experiential counterpart to the scriptural *sākṣī* and the rational *dṛk.*

IV

Another way of approaching Advaita Vedānta experientially is to view the hierarchy of the three states—listed in that order as waking, dreaming and deep sleep—in two different but complementary ways.

One can employ the analysis of the three states in order to indicate both the nature of this pure subject, *and* how it might be discovered. This dual thrust of the fresh analysis of the three states is the clear implication, for instance, of some of the remarks by Ramaṇa Maharṣi. On the one hand, he admits that, in a sense, the state of deep sleep is closer to the state of the pure subject as "the sleep state is free from thoughts and their impression on the individual."[97] Yet, at the same time, he warns that one should not "therefore desire to be always in sleep" because the "incentive to realize" the self "can arise only in the waking state and efforts can only be made when one is awake."[98]

This distinction between what is to be realized and how it is to be realized is crucial to an understanding of the way these three states of waking, dreaming and deep sleep are approached in experiential Advaita. In effect, Ramaṇa, and earlier thinkers of Advaita, set up these three states in a pattern of opposing hierarchies (somewhat like structure and anti-structure). One may designate them as a theoretical and the practical approaches to the issue. "The theoretical approach shows us where we want to go, i.e., to the interiorisation and the unification of consciousness, while the practical approach indicates the means to achieve that end, i.e., through Advaitic knowledge or yogic will."[99]

The theoretical approach may be elaborated first. It could be argued that as one moves from the waking states progressively to dreaming and deep sleep in the world of ordinary experience, consciousness becomes increasingly rarefied in the empirical subject. In the waking state, objects are experienced in the external world. In the dreaming state, objects become a product of the person's interior consciousness. In deep sleep, the distinction between the subject and the object dissolves—even the internal division within a dream between the experiencing subject and the experienced object vanishes. All that is left is the sleeping person. But as on waking up the person remembers having slept, there must have been some conscious subject that witnessed the unconsciousness of sleep. This pure subject has to be realized. Its realization is said to put an end to all unhappiness. Such is the Advaitin claim, that except for one who experientially comes to "know" this pure subject, which is known solely by means of itself "on account of its self-luminosity", according to Ramaṇa "every man, from king to peasant has a certain account of sorrow. Even in cases where it seems absent it is only a time factor that makes you think so —sooner or later it comes."[100] That is, until Self-realization is achieved.

This analysis is suggestive in several ways. First, it suggests that a radical discontinuity is involved in realizing the pure subject, on account of its purity: its total absence of any relationship with any object as in deep sleep, as distinguished from its interiorised relationship as in dreams or an external relation as in the waking state. Thus the knowledge of the pure subject is categorically different from the knowledge or absence of it which arises in a subject-object context, even though this latter type of knowledge is itself qualitatively different in waking, dreaming and deep sleep. Second, as the realization of pure subjectivity entails the total elimination of any form of object-contextuality, the realization of the pure subject is a purely negative enterprise, in the sense that all objects have to be eliminated at all levels—including the possibility of a subject in a state of *relation* to no objects. The subject must be just that. "When non-self disappears, the self alone remains. To make room it is enough that cramping is removed. Space is not brought in afresh. Say more space is there even in cramping."[101] This passage serves to explain the comment that while in ordinary experience the "true self-cannot be known, it doesn't therefore remain unrealized, for it is self-revealing. In fact it can never be wholly suppressed."[102] It is in this sense perhaps that one must understand Ramaṇa's remark: "The feeling that I have not realized is the obstruction to realization. In fact, it is already realized..."""[103]

The practical approach toward the realization of the self and its relation to the three states of waking, dreaming and deep sleep may now be examined. Any effort at realization involves volition, so from a practical point of view the hierarchy must now be reversed: no volition is possible in deep sleep, perhaps more in dreaming but most in the waking state.

The overall point may be graphically presented as follows:

Deep Sleep	Waking
Dreaming	Dreaming
Waking	Deep Sleep
The three states in terms of unification of consciousness	The three states in terms of degrees of volition in Consciousness

The special point to note is that one cannot just jump from one pyramid to the other. It is somewhat like the experience in mountaineering, when we may be standing on a cliff atop one mountain and within close reach of another mountain. It would be foolhardy, however, to just try to jump from the top of a cliff on to the other mountain. One must come down all the way and then climb to the top of the other.

V

What, it might be asked, is the exact nature of the problem towards solving which efforts must be directed in the waking state?

The problem is best illustrated with the help of an example. Let us take the case of a young lady who is in love with her *beau* and goes out to buy a nice dress to please him. She brings that dress home and places it on the table. She then reclines on the chair and begins to speculate on the romantic possibilities this addition to her wardrobe could set in motion.

She imagines how she will wear the dress in the evening and go out for a candle-lit dinner with her friend. She will iron the dress with particular care and wear a perfume with it. She imagines the possibility of spilling wine on it and spoiling the dress (God forbid), and how she will preserve it and after years of marriage still keep it though it may be worn out by then, and how she will show it to her daughter as the dress she wore on the evening her husband proposed to her. While she is thus thinking, the phone rings and she talks to her friend about this fabulous dress she bought in the morning, describing in great detail the way it came to be purchased.

Throughout this series of events the actual dress has simply been lying on the table. So all her experiences don't really pertain to the dress but to the dress-thought. When she thinks of wearing the dress it is really the dress-thought she is concerned with—the dress as such is merely lying on the table. The web of romantic associations she has woven are also woven not around the dress itself, which just lies as an item on the table, but around the dress-thought, in her mind. When she talks with her friend on the phone she really talks of the dress-thought, not the dress itself, which lies on the table and is indifferent to the vicissitudes of fortune the dress-thought is undergoing. The moment the lady stops thinking or talking of the dress-thought—which is what is really involved in the thinking or talking about it rather than the dress itself—the dress-thought may be said to go back into the dress.

This example serves to illustrate several aspects of the problem at hand. It is the Advaitin contention that what we are concerned with in the process of ordinary living is not the real *I* but the *I-thought,* just as what the lady was concerned with in exploring her romantic situation was the dress-thought and not the dress, even though she may find it difficult to draw this distinction. Although the dress as dress-thought was the object of so much activity, the dress as such just lay passively on the table. It is the Advaitin contention that just as it was not the dress but the dress-thought which ran the young lady's life for a while, it is not pure subject—the pure *I*—but the *I- thought* which runs our lives, divorced from the real *I* but deriving its existence from it, just as the dress-thought is divorced from the dress and yet derives its existence from it! This *I-thought* is also called the ego and it is said that "those alone who have found out the real nature of the ego have seen reality. They will have no more doubts or anxiety."[104] Even this point can be clarified analogically:

just as once one has discovered the nature of the dress-thought—which one constantly confused with the dress itself—one would also discover the real nature of the dress as such, unclouded by the dress-thought.

In Advaita, it is said that realization of one's true nature entails realizing how the *I-thought* rises from the real *I*. "To say *I am this* or *I am that* there must be the *I*. This *I* is only the ego or the *I-thought* is therefore the root-thought ...find out its source. Then all these [other thoughts] will vanish and the pure self will remain over."[105] Similarly one is told that the ego proceeds from the self as a spark from fire. "The spark is called the ego. In the case of the ignorant man it identifies itself with an object simultaneously with its rise. It cannot remain independent of such association with objects If its objectifying tendency is killed it remains pure and also merges into the source."[106] This point can also be made in relation to the analogy of the dress-thought and the dress. When we perceive the dress *qua* dress without dress-thoughts, one can describe the process as either tracing dress-thoughts back to their source, the dress, or making dress-thoughts merge into the dress.

Just as one needed to distinguish between the dress and the dress-thought, one needs to distinguish between the *I* and the *I-thought*. "You must distinguish between the *I*, pure in itself, and the *I*- thought."[107] "If you stay as the *I*, your being alone, without thought, the *I*-thought will disappear and the delusion will vanish forever."[108]

This raises the interesting question: are there two *I*s ? The parallel question in terms of the analogy would be—are there two dresses ? There is only one dress. Similarly, there is only one *I*. But just as the dress gives rise to the dress-thought, the *I-thought* emerges from the *I*. Or, one can even say that once the dress-thought has arisen, several dress-thoughts in various phases arise based on the original dress-thought. Thus the sequence runs as follows: dress > dress-thought > dress thought*s*. This helps explain the following: "The *I* of the dream has vanished. Another *I* speaks of the dream.

This *I* was not in the dream. Both the *I*'s are unreal. There is the substratum of the mind which continues all along, giving rise to so many scenes. With every thought rises *I*, and with its disappearance the *I* disappears too. So the *I*s are born, and die every moment,"[109] like dress-thoughts emerging from moment to moment. Once one knows that the dress is lying safely on the table the vicissitudes of the dress-thoughts cease to be a cause for concern.

There are other ways as well in which the analogy of the dress and dress-thought is illuminating. For instance, it is said in Advaita : "That which makes the enquiry is the ego. The *I* about which the inquiry is made is also the ego. As a result of the enquiry the ego ceases to exist."[110] Parallel: starting as we do from the realm of the dress-thought, it is the dress-thought, which inquires into itself. Then it realizes it is just the dress-thought and disappears, yielding place to the actual dress lying on the table. Again, in Advaita one is encouraged to enquire who undergoes the vicissitudes of life and discover that only the ego is affected by them, not the self, and that "the ego is non-existent." Parallel: the dress-thoughts undergo all the vicissitudes, they do not bind the dress itself and the dress-thoughts are non-existent in the sense that what really exists is only the dress. Again it is said: "Reality is simply the loss of ego."[111] Parallel : the recognition of the reality of the dress is simply the loss of dress-thoughts. Thus the analogy is helpful in many ways. Let me close by pointing out two more instances in which it is helpful in a much more dynamic sense—in shedding light on the actual pursuit of the spiritual goal.

It is sometimes said that the realization could be sudden or gradual, that is, taking time to steady itself. At times Ramaṇa said that "there are no degrees of liberation,"[112] and at other times that "realization takes time to steady itself."[113] This could also be understood in terms of our analogy. Let us imagine that the young lady in the parable is suddenly told that her *beau* has run off with someone else! If the lady is shocked to her sense by this revelation the dress would immediately become a piece of cloth for her—the dress-thoughts would disappear. If, however, she still retained affection for the heel who left her, dress-thoughts might still occasionally arise from the dress and may only gradually subside till the dress become just a piece of cloth (that is, till she finds another *beau*).

It is also sometimes said that realization is not possible so long as one is "aware of an *I*"; it is only possible upon "being the *I*". So long as one has thoughts of the dress, one is in a sense in a state of alienation from the dress and still in the realm of dress-thoughts. But when the dress becomes the dress —that is, when all dress-thought disappear, then alone it is in its natural and primal state.

The process of realization may be said to consist of three stages. In the first stage one is aware of only the *I-thought* to begin with. One is so carried away by this identification with the *I-thought* to begin with that one doesn't know there is an underlying real *I* which is quite different from the *I-thought*, although the source of it. In other words, the pure subject, though ever present, is never known because of one's identification of existence with the three states of consciousness which conceal the pure witness. One must, in the second stage, lose sight of the world to experience the pure subject. As Ramaṇa explains in this catechetical series:

> When will the realization of the self be gained ? When the world, which is what is seen as, has been removed, there will be realization of the self which is the seer.
>
> Will there not be the realization of the self—even while the world is there (taken as real)? There will not be.[114]

In the third stage, once the pure subject is realized, the world is again seen but now as part of the self and not apart from it as was the case in the beginning. In terms of our analogy one begins with the young lady with her mind full of dress-thoughts. In stage two she experiences the actual dress to be worn. She cannot see it unless the dress-thoughts depart from the mind, so that she can see and experience the actual dress. While actually experiencing it even the thought "this is the dress" is a distraction from it. Finally, emerging from the absorption in the dress she can again lose herself in dress-thoughts going down the aisle but she is aware of the relationship of these dress thoughts to the real dress, which was not the case the first time.

The relation between the dress and the dress-thought continues to possess considerable illustrative and therefore explanatory power. This becomes apparent, when we explore the nature of the *I*-thought as analyzed in Advaita Vedānta a little further. When the "I" thought arises in the context of person, it is worth noting that it often takes the form "I-am-the-body".[115] That is to say—it is not a vague free-floating "I" thought and it has a definite if fully undetermined referent. Similarly, the dress-thought, in relation to the dress, is not a dress thought in general, but assumes the form of "*a* dress-thought" rather than "dress thought" in general, or a collection of dresses as it were. "Is there not a name for the body? It is that which we take as the name of that particular person. When asked who you are, one says, *I am Rāma.* If someone calls *Rāma,* that person alone looks back. While other bodies have other names, this particular body becomes Rāma"[116] Similarly, other chains of dress thoughts may have their own identities, and may arise in different contexts, but this chain of dress-thought possesses its own identity—and destiny.

The metaphor on hand can even be developed to indicate the relation between the various sheaths mentioned in the Upaniṣads, and its relation to the *I* and the *I-thought.* In accordance with the doctrine of the various *kośas* or sheaths, an individual is presented as "sheathed" in five of them—and at their core lies the true ātman or *I.* But empirically, the person exists as an entity covered in these sheaths and generated by an "I-thought". The person is like the young lady wrapped up in the dress, but still carried away by the "dress-thought" into the reverie she is in. In fact one can come to point even more directly here, by undertaking a simple exercise. Please sit down at a desk quietly and just think of yourself as someone sitting down by the desk quietly. What you have in your mind is an *I-thought* of yourself sitting down by the desk. Similarly, the young lady sitting by herself thinking of doing all kinds of things with the dress on, is trafficking in the *dress-thought* just as we traffic in *I-thought.*

Experiential Advaita also draws a distinction between what is called *manolaya* and *manonāśa.* The first term stands for the temporary suspension of mental activity and the second term for final elimination of mental activity as an obstacle to self-realization. The distinction is important in experiential Advaita because it is on the basis of this distinction that it distinguishes its own *samādhi* from that which results from the practice of Yoga. Ramaṇa Maharṣi explains the point as follows:

> In deep sleep the mind is merged and not destroyed. That which merges reappears. It may happen in meditation also. But the mind which is destroyed cannot reappear. The yogi's aim must be to destroy it and not to sink into *laya.* In the peace of meditation, *laya* sometimes ensues but it is not enough. It must be supplemented by other practices for destroying the mind. Some people have gone into yogic *samādhi* with a trifling thought and after a long time awakened in the trail of the same thought. In the meantime generations have passed in the world. Such a yogi has not destroyed his mind. The true destruction of the mind is the non- recognition of it as being apart from the Self.[117]

The metaphor of the dress is useful here. So long as the idea of the wedding persists, the dress-thoughts will continue to reappear even if they disappear for a while, but once the idea of wedding is abandoned altogether, the dress-thoughts will cease and stop interfering with one's perception of the dress as such.

We often talk of the mind. It is one of the claims of experiential Advaita that the concept the mind doesn't bear scrutiny.

> What is the mind? The reply which Bhagavān [Ramaṇa Maharṣi] gives us is that mind is nothing but (a bundle of) thoughts. If one investigates what this mind is, keeping off all thoughts, he will find that there is no such thing as mind.[118]

The link between the *I* and the *I-thought* is the mind. When it is claimed that there is no mind what is meant is that there is no mind apart from the thoughts, just as there is no river apart from its flow. Similarly, then, there is no *dress-thought* apart from the bundle of thoughts which have arisen from the dress or flow from it. And further: just as if one probed these "dress-thoughts" uninterruptedly one will be led back to the dress, so also the uninterrupted interrogation of I-thoughts will jolt one back to the true *I*.

At another level the whole metaphor of the dress and dress-thought in a way helps elaborate the way the subtle body is said to operate in the psychology of Advaita Vedānta. The following account is self-explanatory in this respect.

> Let it not be considered that the mind takes a subtle body only in dreams. The same phenomenon takes place even in the waking state during flights of the mind, for instance in a revery. Suppose we sit and imagine in the waking state that we travel to far off countries, meet a friend there, talk with him or undergo all the vicissitudes of life. The mentally projected body in which we seem to undergo all these experiences is also our subtle body. We know that these subtle bodies we take up now and then are transient. When one wakes

> up from a dream, the dream body is gone. In the same way the body assumed in day-dreams (reveries) is also found to be false, i.e. these bodies are the false forms that come to and go away from us. Because we exist even in the absence of these bodies, they are not WE.[119]

In the course of developing this illustration so far we have focused on the emergence of the dress-thought (and then even dress-thoughts) from the dress as an example of how the I-thought (and then even the many I-thoughts) can arise from the real "I". With a little shift in focus, however, the application of this I metaphor to our existential situation can also be enlarged. In order to see how this might be possible let's go back to the young lady who imagines wearing the dress she has bought when she goes out with her *beau* for the candle-light dinner.

Let us now visualize her imagining this scene while relaxing in her room—that she is sitting next to her *beau* on a table in the restaurant in the dress she has bought. Now note that not only is she *wearing* a dress-thought as she imagines herself in the restaurant, she herself, as she imagines herself in the restaurant, is not she herself but a *thought* of herself. For she, as she really is, is sitting right there in the room! So it is a she-thought (and not she, although the she-thought proceeds from her) who is wearing the dress-thought! Now note that the dress-thought is an *object* and she-thought is a *subject*, and the *she*-thought is also wearing the *dress*-thought—that is—the object and subject are interacting but in a world of *thought*—so that their interaction also partakes of the same character. The ontological status of all of them, though derivative, is the same! This is how Advaita Vedānta is able to combine an empirical realism with a transcendental idealism.

Or to put the matter more philosophically: a major issue this school of thought has to contend with is not an unexpected one: how to reconcile its claim of a metaphysical non-dual reality with the apparent plurality of our empirical existence.

Here is a glimpse of the ways in which such a reconciliation might be proposed. The range of our experience in the empirical world is vertiginously diverse, but a little reflection suggests that all of it occurs in one of three states of consciousness: when one is awake, when one is dreaming and while one is in deep sleep. These three states of experience provide a useful handle for talking of our empirical world because all the varied experiences we have in this world can be slotted as falling within one of these three states of consciousness. Now in the waking state physical objects are real (at the empirical level). It can thus be described as *sat* or real. Compared to them objects and persons encountered in a dream are merely mental in nature and it can thus be described as *cit*, or characterized by immaterial conscious-ness. Finally, the experience of deep sleep is universally considered restful, blissful and happy. Thus this state of consciousness qualifies as *ānanda* or bliss. Thus the empirical reality we experience can be described as follows:

Waking	Sat
Dreaming	Cit
Deep Sleep	Ānanda

Readers will recall, however, that the ultimate reality, at the transcendental level, was also described in part I of this book as *saccidānanda Brahman*, where *Brahman* denoted the ultimate reality to which the words *sat* (reality), *cit* (consciousness) and *ānanda* (bliss) are applied as ways of orienting ourselves towards it.

In other words, the question we are dealing with may be rephrased as follows: what is the relationship of the ultimate reality as *sat, cit* and *ānanda* and our experience of the empirical world, which is also capable of being so described.

The question may be answered with the help of a chart.

Sat, Cit, Ānanda, Brahman

Sat	Waking	
Cit	Dreaming	World
Ānanda	Deep Sleep	

How could the horizontal line become the vertical, in other words? Just as a straight rod appears bent when placed in a tub full of water, say Advaita Vedānta. That is to say, there is something in the nature of the empirical world which apparently distorts the ultimate reality when viewed in relation with it. The word used to denote this *something* in Advaita Vedānta is *māyā* or *avidyā.*

But matters get straightened out when one achieves enlightenment. One way of moving towards such enlightenment or Realisation is to ask the question: if I undergo the experience of waking, dreaming and deep sleep which as states of consciousness differ so radically from one another, then how do I retain my sense of identity despite undergoing these different states of experience, and the different experiences I have within these states of waking, dreaming and deep sleep. There must be some *unchanging* consciousness in me which undergirds my consciousness of *change* of these states of consciousness and the changes within them. Such unchanging consciousness is called *ātman* in Advaita Vedānta—which constitutes the unchanging core of our being.

According to Advaita Vedānta this *ātman* is identical with *Brahman.* They are not two. It is this understanding of non-dualism—that the *ātman* and *Brahman* are not two distinct entities but identically one—which represents experientially the most resonant dimension of Advaitic non-dualism. This is the truth but somehow it has become warped and it is the goal of Advaita Vedānta to help us straighten it out.

VI

In analysing the experiential approach so far we have stuck to the experience of ordinary human beings. It may not be out of place now at least to refer to the experiences of an extraordinary kind which have a bearing on Advaita Vedānta.

We have some accounts of mystical experiences of the Advaitic variety from the accounts of the lives of mystics of the twentieth century, which bear on the present discussion.

They are such as are best shared rather than explained.

The first of these is from the life of Swāmī Vivekānanda (1863-1902) who bore the name Narendra Nath Dutt, or Naren for short, before he became a monk. He ultimately came to acknowledge Śrī Rāmakṛṣṇa Paramhaṁsa(1836-1886) as his master. The relevance of the following account of a spiritual incident between the two will not be lost on students of Advaita Vedānta.

> Thus one day the Master told Narendranath many things indicating the oneness of Jīva and Brahman of the non-dual philosophy. He heard those words, undoubtedly with attention, but he could not comprehend them and went to Hazra at the end of the Master's talk. Smoking and discussing those things again with Hazra, he said, 'Can it ever be possible that the waterpot is God, the cup is God, whatever we see and all of us are God?' Shri Hazra also joined Narendra in thus ridiculing the idea and both of them burst into laughter. The Master was till then in the state of partial external consciousness. Hearing Narendra laugh, he came out of his room like a boy with his wearing cloth in his armpit and, coming to them smiling, said affectionately, 'What are you both talking about?' He then touched Narendra and went into samādhi.
>
> Narendra said to us afterwards, 'There was a complete revolution in the state of my mind in a moment at the wonderful touch of the Master. I was aghast to see actually that there was nothing in the whole universe except God. But I remained silent in spite of seeing it, wondering how long that state would last. But that inebriation did not at all diminish that day. I returned home; it was all the same there; it seemed to me that all that I saw was He. I sat far my meal when I saw that all -food,

> plate, the one who was serving as well as myself—were nothing but He. I took a mouthful or two and sat quiet. My mother's affectionate words—"why do you sit quiet; why don't you eat?"—brought me to consciousness and I began eating again. Thus, I had that experience at the time of eating or drinking, sitting or lying, going to the college or taking a stroll. I was always overwhelmed with a sort of indescribable intoxication. When I walked along the streets and saw a carriage coming along before me I did not feel inclined, as at other times, to move away, lest it should collide with me. For, I thought, "I am also that and nothing but that". My hands and feet always remained insensible at that time. I felt no satisfaction whatever when I took my food. It seemed to me as if some one else was eating the meal... When that overwhelming intoxication diminished a little, the world appeared to me to be a dream. Going for a walk on the bank of the Hedua tank, I knocked my head against the iron railings round it to see whether what I saw were dream-rails or actual ones. On account of the insensibility of my hands and feet I was afraid whether I was not going to have paralysis. I could not escape that terrible intoxicating mood and overwhelming condition for some time. When I came to the normal state, I thought that that was indication of non-dual knowledge. So what is written in the *Śāstras* about it is by no means untrue. Since then I could never doubt the truth of non-duality.[120]

The second account is drawn from the life of Ramaṇa Maharṣi (1879-1950) who is regarded as one of the great Advaitins of our age. He underwent the following precocious experience in 1896.

> It was about six weeks before I left Madurai for good

that the great change in my life took place. It was so sudden. One day I sat alone on the first floor of my uncle's house. I was in my usual health. I seldom had any illness. I was a heavy sleeper. When I was at Dindigul in 1891 a huge crowd had gathered close to the room where I slept and tried to rouse me by shouting and knocking at the door, all in vain, and it was only by their getting into my room and giving me a violent shake that I was roused from my torpor. This heavy sleep was rather a proof of good health. I was also subject to fits of half-awake sleep at night. My wily playmates, afraid to trifle with me when I was awake, would go to me when I was asleep, rouse me, take me all round the playground, beat me, cuff me, sport with me, and bring me back to my bed—and all the while I would put up with everything with a meekness, humility, forgiveness, and passivity unknown to my waking state. When the morning broke I had no remembrance of the night's experiences. But these fits did not render me weaker or less fit for life and were hardly to be considered a disease. So, on that day as I sat alone there was nothing wrong with my health. But sudden and unmistakable fear of death seized me. I felt I was going to die. Why I should have so felt cannot now be explained by anything felt in my body. Nor could I explain it to myself then. I did not however trouble myself to discover if the fear was well grounded. I felt *I was going to die*, and at once set about thinking out what I should do. I did not care to consult doctors or elders or even friends. I felt I had to solve the problem myself then and there.

The shock of fear of death made me at once introspective, or *introverted*. I said to myself mentally, i.e., without uttering the words—'Now, death has come. What does it mean? What is it that is dying?

This body dies.' I at once dramatised the scene of death. I extended my limbs and held them rigid as though *rigor-mortis* had set in. I imitated a corpse to lend an air of reality to my further investigation, I held my breath and kept my mouth closed, pressing the lips together so that no sound might escape. Let not the word I or any other word be uttered! *Well then,* said I to myself, 'this body is dead. It will be carried stiff to the burning ground and there burnt and reduced to ashes. But with the death of this body, am "I" dead? Is the body "I"? This body is silent and inert. But I feel the full force of my personality and even the sound "I" within myself,—apart from the body. So "I" am a spirit, a thing transcending the body. The material body dies, but the spirit transcending it cannot be touched by death. I am therefore the deathless spirit.' All this was not a mere intellectual process, but flashed before me vividly as living truth, something which I perceived immediately, without any argument almost. *I* was something very real, the only real thing in that state, and all the conscious activity that was connected with my body was centred on that. The *I* or my *self* was holding the focus of attention by a powerful fascination from that time forwards. Fear of death had vanished at once and forever. Absorption in the self has continued from that moment right up to this time. Other thoughts may come and go like the various notes of a musician, but the *I* continues like the basic or fundamental *śruti* note which accompanies and blends with all other notes. Whether the body was engaged in talking, reading, or anything else, I was still centred on *I*. Previous to that crisis I had no clear perception of myself and was not consciously attracted to it. I had felt no direct perceptible interest in it, much less any

> permanent disposition to dwell upon it. The consequences of this new habit were soon noticed in my life.[121]

Paul Brunton offers the following abbreviated account.

> Maharṣi told once how he got realization. On the day his father died he felt puzzled by death and pondered over it, whilst his mother and brothers wept. He thought for hours and after the corpse was cremated he got by analysis to the point of perceiving that it was the *I* which makes the body to see, to run, to walk and to eat. "I now know this *I* but my father's *I* has left the body".[122]

The third account is the report of a talk by J. Krishnamurti (1895-1986). Whether Krishnamurti should be installed in the Advaitic pantheon is a matter of debate, therefore a word of explanation might be required by way justifying the inclusion of the excerpt. One of the chief tenets of Advaita Vedānta, as scripturally propounded, is the claim that realization is achieved not by action (*karma*) but *jñāna* (insight); that what transcends action cannot be achieved by action. The following discourse of Krishnamurti is potentially illuminating in this respect.

> *Krishnamurti*: For most of us, our whole life is based on effort, some kind of volition. And we cannot conceive of an action that is not based on it. Our social, economic, and so-called spiritual life, is a series of efforts, always culminating in a certain result. We think effort is essential. So we are now going to find out if it is possible to live differently, without this constant battle.
>
> Why do we make effort? Put simply, it is in order to achieve a result, to become something, to reach a goal, isn't it? If we do not make an effort, we think we shall stagnate. We have an idea about the goal towards which we are constantly striving;

and this striving has become part of our life. If we want to alter, to bring about a radical change in ourselves, we make a tremendous effort to eliminate old habits, to resist the habitual environmental influences, and so on. So we are used to this series of efforts in order to find or achieve something, in order to live at all.

Now, is not all such effort the activity of the self? Is not effort self-centred activity? And, if we make an effort from the centre of the self, it must inevitably produce more conflict, more confusion, more misery. Yet we keep on making effort after effort; and very few of us realize that the self-centred activity of effort does not clear up any of our problems. On the contrary, it increases our confusion and our misery and our sorrow. Or we know this, and yet continue hoping somehow to break through this self-centred activity of effort, the action of the will.

This is our problem—Is it possible to understand anything without effort? Is it possible to see what is real, what is true, without introducing the action of the will, which is essentially based on the self, the *me*? And if we do not make an effort, is there not a danger of deterioration, of going to sleep, of stagnation? Perhaps, as I am talking, we can experiment with this individually, and see how far we can go through this question. For I feel that what brings happiness, quietness, tranquillity of the mind, does not come through any effort. A truth is not perceived through any volition, through any action of will. And if we can go into it very carefully and diligently, perhaps we shall find the answer.

How do we react when a truth is presented? Take, for example, the problem of fear. We realize that our activity and our being and our whole existence would be fundamentally altered if there was no fear of any kind in us. We may see that, we may see the truth of it; and thereby there is freedom from fear. But for most of us, when a fact, a truth, is put before us, what is our immediate response? Please, experiment with what I am saying; please do not merely listen. Watch your own reactions; and find out what happens when a truth, a fact, is out before you—such as 'any dependence in relationship destroys relationship'. Now, when a statement of that kind is made, what is your response? Do you see, are you aware of, the truth of it, and does dependency thereby cease? Or have you an idea about the fact? Here is a statement of truth. Do we experience the truth of it, or do we create an idea about it?

If we can understand this process of the creation of idea, then we shall perhaps understand the whole process of effort. Because once we have created the idea, then effort comes into being. Then the problem arises, what to do, how to act? That is, we see that psychological dependence on another is a form of self-fulfilment; it is not love; in it there is conflict, fear, the desire to fulfil oneself through another, jealousy, and so on, which corrode. We see that psychological dependence on another embraces all these facts. Then, we proceed to create the idea, do we not? We do not directly experience the fact, the truth of it; but, we look at it, and then create an idea of how to be free from dependence. We see the implications of psychological dependence, and then we create the idea of how to be free from it. We do not directly experience the truth, which is the liberating factor. But out of the experience of looking at that fact we create an idea. We are incapable of looking at it directly, without ideation.

Then, having created the idea, we proceed to carry out that idea into action. Then we try to bridge the gap between idea and action—in which effort is involved.

So can we not look at the truth without creating ideas? It is almost instinctive with most of us: when something true is out before us, we immediately create an idea about it. And I think if we can understand why we do this so instinctively, almost unconsciously, then perhaps we shall understand if it is possible to be free from effort.

Why then do we create ideas about truth? Surely that is important to find out, is it not? Either we see the truth nakedly, as it is, or we do not. But why do we have a picture about it, a symbol, a word, an image, which necessitates a postponement, the hope of an eventual result? So can we hesitantly and guardedly go into this process of why the mind creates the image, the idea—that I must be this or that, that I must be free from dependence, and so on? We know very well that when we see something very clearly, experience it directly, there is a freedom from it. It is that immediacy that is vital, not the picture or the symbol of the truth—on which all systems and philosophies and deteriorating organizations are built. So is it not important to find out why the mind, instead of seeing the thing directly and simply, and experiencing the truth of it immediately, creates an idea about it?

I do not know if you have thought about this. It may perhaps be something new. And to find the truth of it, please do not merely resist. Do not say, 'What would happen if the mind did not create the idea? It is its function to create ideas, to verbalize, to recall memories, to recognize, to calculate'. We know that. But the mind is not free; and it is only when the mind is capable of looking at the truth totally, completely, without any barrier, that there is freedom.

So our problem is—why does the mind, instead of seeing the thing immediately and experiencing it directly, indulge in all these ideas. Is this not one of the habits of the mind? Something is presented to us, and immediately there is the old habit of creating an idea, a theory about it. And the mind likes to live in habit. Because without habit the mind is lost. If there is not a routine, a habitual response to which it has become accustomed, it feels confused, uncertain.

That is one aspect. Also, does not the mind seek a result? Because in the result is permanence. And the mind hates to be uncertain. It is always seeking security in different forms—through beliefs, through knowledge, through experience. And when that is questioned there is a disturbance, anxiety. And so the mind, avoiding uncertainty, seeks security for itself by making efforts to achieve a result.

I hope you are actually observing your own minds in operation. If you are not, then you will not experience, your mind will remain on the verbal level. But—if I may suggest—if you can observe your own mind in operation, and watch how it thinks, how it reacts, when a truth is out before it, then you will experience step-by-step what I am talking about. Then there will be an extraordinary experience. And it is this direct approach, this direct experience of what truth is that is so essential for bringing about a creative life.

So why does the mind create these ideas, instead of directly experiencing? Why does the mind intervene? As we have said, it is habit. Also, the mind wants to achieve a result. We all want to achieve a result. In listening to me, are you looking for a result? You are, aren't you? The mind is seeking a result; it sees that dependence is destructive, and therefore it wants to be free of it. But the very desire to be free creates the idea. The mind is not free; but the desire to be free creates the idea of freedom as the goal towards which it must work. And thereby effort comes into being. And that effort is self-centred; it does not bring freedom. Instead of depending on a person, you depend on an idea or on an image. So your effort is only self-enclosing; it is not liberating.

Now, can the mind, realizing that it is caught in habit, be free from habit—not have an idea that it should achieve freedom as an eventual goal, but see the truth that the mind is caught in habit, directly experience it? And, similarly, can the mind see that it is pursuing incessantly a permanence for itself, a goal that it must achieve, a God, a truth, a virtue, a state of being, or whatever, and is thereby bringing about this action of will, with all its complications? And when we see that, is it not possible to experience the truth of something *directly* without all the paraphernalia of verbalization? You may objectively see a fact, in that there is no ideation, no creation of idea, symbol, desire. But subjectively, inwardly, it is entirely different. Because there we want a result; there is the craving to be something, to achieve, to become—in which all effort is born.

I feel that to see what is true from moment to moment, without any effort, but directly to experience it, is the only creative existence. Because it is only in moments of complete tranquillity that you discover something—not when you are making an effort, whether it is under the microscope or inwardly. It is only when the mind is not agitated, not caught in habit, not trying to achieve a result, not trying to become something—it is only when it is not doing these things, when it is really tranquil, when there is no effort, no movement—that there is a possibility of discovering something new.

Surely, that is freedom from the self, that is the abnegation of the *me*—and not the outward symbols, whether you possess this or that virtue or not. But freedom comes into being only when you understand your own processes, conscious as well as unconscious. It is possible only when we go fully into the different processes of the mind. And as most of us live in a state of tension, in constant effort, it is essential to understand the complexity of effort, to see the truth that effort does not bring virtue, that effort is not love, that effort does not bring about the freedom that truth alone can give—which is direct experiencing. For that, one has to understand the mind, one's own mind—not somebody else's mind, not what somebody else says about it. You may read all the volumes ever written but they will be utterly useless. For you must observe your own mind, and penetrate it more and more deeply, and experience the thing directly as you go along. Because *there* is the living quality, not in the things of the mind. And the mind, to find its own processes, must not be enclosed by its own habits, but must be free occasionally to look. Therefore, it is important to understand this whole process of effort. For effort does not bring about freedom. Effort is only more and more self-enclosing, more and more destructive, outwardly as well as inwardly, in relationship with one or with many.[123]

Conclusion

A verse, popular in India, claims to summarize the teachings of the school of Advaita Vedānta in just half of a verse:

> Brahman is real; the world is an illusory appearance;
> and the individual soul (*jīva*) [in its true character]
> is Brahman alone, none other.[124]

Or to put the matter more formally:

> The non-duality of *Brahman*, the non-reality of the world, and the non-difference of the soul [*Ātman*] from Brahman—these constitute the teaching of Advaita.[125]

The reader would have noticed that whether we approach Advaita Vedānta scripturally, or rationally, or experientially, in the end one finds oneself face-to-face with the pedagogical structure which bears a family-resemblance to this statement.

While following the scriptural approach one starts out with Brahman and Ātman and has to confront the issue of their identity in the face of the apparent plurality which characterizes our life. In adopting the rational approach one starts out with the world—or an object of the world—and finds oneself confronting indeterminate existence. In adopting the experiential approach one starts out with oneself only to see one's self facing experiential dissolution. In all three cases one finds oneself at an interface between reality and unreality—but an unreality which cannot be severed from Reality and vice versa, as it were.

The aim of this book was not much to convey the technical details of the system of philosophy of Advaita Vedānta, on which many books exist, as to convey its spirit, for it is as much a spirituality as a philosophy. Whether it has succeeded in this is for the reader to decide.

Notes

1. Andrew O. Fort, *Jivanmukti in Transformation: Embodied Liberation in Advaita and Neo-Vedānta* (Albany, N.Y.: State University of New York Press, 1998).
2. Wilhelm Halbfass, *India and Europe: An Essay in Understanding* (Albany, N.Y.: State University of New York Press, 1988) p. 353.
3. M. Hiriyanna, *The Essentials of Indian Philosophy*, (London: George Allen & Unwin, 1949) p. 19.
4. *Ibid.*, p. 152.
5. *Ibid.*, p. 154.
6. For a good discussion of this point see John Grimes, *Problems and Perspectives in Religious Discourse: Advaita Vedānta Implications* (Albany, N.Y.: State University of New York Press, 1994).
7. *Ibid.*, p. 156-157.
8. *Ibid*, p. 157-158.
9. *Ibid*, p. 158.
10. *Ibid.*
11. *Ibid.*, p. 157.
12. *Ibid.*, p. 158.
13. *Ibid.*
14. *Ibid.*, p. 47-48.
15. *Ibid.*, p. 159-160.
16. K. Satchidananda Murty, *Revelation and Reason in Advaita Vedānta.* (Delhi: Motilal Banarsidass, 1974) p. 40.
17. M. Hiriyanna, *Indian Philosophical Studies.* (Mysore: Kavyalaya Publishers, 1957) p. 89.
18. M. Hiriyanna, *The Essentials of Indian Philosophy*, p. 21.
19. *Ibid.*
20. Robert Ernest Hume, tr. *The Thirteen Principal Upanishads.* (London: Oxford University Press, 1968) p. 113-114.
21. Thomas J. Hopkins, *The Hindu Religious Tradition* (Encino, California and Belmont, California: Dickenson Publishing Company, Inc., 1971) p. 37.
22. Robert Ernest Hume, tr., *op. cit.*, p, 132-133.

23. Ainslie T. Embree, ed., *Sources of Indian Tradition* (second edition) (New York: Columbia University Press, 1988) Vol. I, p. 32.
24. *Ibid.*, p. 33
25. *Ibid.*
26. S. Radhakrishnan, *The Principal Upaniṣads.* (Atlantic Heights, NJ: Humanities Press, 1992) p. 695-705.
27. *Ibid.*, p. 36.
28. Ainslie T. Embree, ed., *The Hindu Tradition* (New York: Random House, 1972) p. 52.
29. *Ibid.*, p. 55.
30. *Ibid.*, p. 55.
31. *Ibid*, p. 21.
32. *Ibid.*, p. 22.
33. *Ibid.*, p. 22.
34. *Ibid.*
35. Troy Wilson Organ, *Hinduism: Its Historical Development* (Woodbury, N.Y.: Barron's Educational Series, 1974) p. 114.
36. M. Hiriyanna, *Outlines of Indian Philosophy*, p. 378.
37. Troy Wilson Organ, *Hinduism: Its Historical Development*, p. 114.
38. *Ibid.*, p.114-115.
39. Chandradhar Sharma, *A Critical Survey of Indian Philosophy* (London: Rider, 1960) p. 282-283.
40. I incorporate material here, which also appears in Arvind Sharma, *The Philosophy of Religion and Advaita Vedānta: A Comparative Study of Religion and Reason* (University Park, Pennsylvania: The Pennsylvania State University Press, 1995) p. 97-99.
41. Satchidananda Murty, *Revelation and Reason in Advaita Vedānta*, p. 81.
42. Robert Ernest Hume, *op. cit.* p. 240-241.
43. See the discussion of the Honey-Doctrine (*madhu-vidyā*), R.E. Hume, *op. cit.*, p. 102-105.
44. M. Hiriyanna, *The Essentials of Indian Philosophy*, p. 157.
45. Heinrich Zimmer, *Philosophies of India.* (Edited by Joseph Campbell. New York: Princeton University Press, 1969) p. 337-338.
46. Patrick Olivelle, *The Early Upaniṣads* (New York: Oxford University Press, 1998) p. 561.
47. S. Radhakrishnan, ed., *op. cit.*, p. 462.
48. *Ibid.*, p. 463.
49. Franklin Edgerton, "Studies in the Veda", *Journal of the American Oriental Society* 35:242 (1915).
50. In the case of some ordeals it is possible to propose a psychological basis for the confidence that the innocent party may get acquitted, although it is doubtful if it applies here:

Specially interesting is the ordeal of the ploughshare, in which the accused man had to touch a red-hot iron ploughshare with his tongue; if it was not burned he was deemed innocent—psychologically a fairly sound test of his own confidence in the result, since if he had a guilty conscience his salivary glands would not function properly, and his tongue would be burnt." (A.L. Basham, *The Wonder that was India* [New Delhi: Rupa & Co., 1999] p.117.) Curiously enough, a similar claim is made in a similar context in Islamic mysticism, as in the Upaniṣadic passage, see Reynold A. Nicholson, *The Mystics of Islam* (Harmondsworth: Penguin, 1889 [1914]) p. 182-183.

51. *Ibid.*, p. 245-250, with subheadings removed.
52. Sacchidananda Murty, *op. cit.*, p. 89.
53. *Ibid.*, Chapter VI passim.
54. *Ibid.*, p. 89-90, 97.
55. *Ibid.*, p. 92.
56. *Ibid.*, p. 93.
57. *Ibid.*, p. 93.
58. *Ibid.*, p. 96.
59. *Ibid.*, p. 98.
60. See Arvind Sharma, *The Philosophy of Religion and Advaita Vedānta: A Comparative Study in Religion and Reason,* p. 46-47.
61. M. Hiriyanna, *The Essentials of Indian Philosophy.* P. 160-161.
62. *Ibid.*, p. 59.
63. *Ibid.*, p. 22-23.
64. Satischandra Chatterjee and Dhirendramohan Datta, *An Introduction to Indian Philosophy* (Calcutta: University of Calcutta, 1950) p. 382.
65. *Ibid.*, p. 382.
66. *Ibid.*
67. *Ibid.*, p. 383.
68. *Ibid.*, p. 383.
69. M. Hiriyanna, *Outlines of Indian Philosophy* (London: George Allen & Unwin, 1932) p. 370.
70. M. Hiriyanna, *Outlines of Indian Philosophy* p. 370-371.
71. Satishchandra Chatterjee and Dhirendramohan Datta, *op. cit.*, p. 383-384.
72. *Ibid.*, p.384.
73. *Ibid.*
74. *Ibid.*, p. 385.
75. *Ibid.*
76. *Ibid.*, diacritics supplied.
77. *Ibid.*, p. 386-387.
78. *Ibid.*, p. 388.

79. *Ibid.*, p. 392.
80. *Ibid.*
81. *Ibid.*, p. 467. "This conclusion is further supported by the linguistic expression 'my body', 'my sense', 'my intellect', 'etc. which show that the self can alienate itself from there (body, sense, etc.) and treat them as external objects distinct from itself. These cannot, therefore, be regarded as the real essence of the self. It is true, one also sometimes says, 'my consciousness.' But such an expression cannot be taken literally, as implying a distinction between the self (as possessor)and consciousness (as possessed). For, if the self tries to distinguish itself from consciousness, it only assumes the form of distinguishing consciousness. Consciousness thus proves inseparable and indistinguishable from the self. So 'my consciousness' must be taken in the metaphorical sense. The possessive case here doesn't really imply distinction, but rather identity or apposition (as in 'The city of London'). By comparing and analyzing the different meanings of the self expressed by 'I' and 'mine' we discover thus pure consciousness as the real essence of the self" *ibid.*, p. 407-408).
82. *Ibid.*, p. 408.
83. M. Hiriyanna, *Indian Philosophical Studies* (Mysore : Kavyalaya Publishers, 1957) p. 135.
84. *Ibid.*, p. 135-136.
85. Satishchandra Chatterjee and Dhirendramohan Datta, *op. cit.*, p. 387.
86. *Ibid.*
87. Quoted in P. Sankaranarayanan, *What is Advaita?* (Bombay: Bharatiya Vidya Bhavan, 1970) p. 46.
88. *Ibid.*, p. 47.
89. Maurice Frydman, tr., *I Am That: Conversations With Sri Nisargadatta Maharaj* (Bombay: Chetana, 1973) Part I, p. 263.
90. John A. Hutchinson, *Paths of Faith* (New York: McGraw-Hill Book Company, 1969) p. 222.
91. Wm. Theodore de Bary ed., *Sources of Chinese Tradition* (New York: Columbia University Press, 1960) Vol. I, p. 73.
92. *Ibid.*, p.72.
93. Ainslie T. Embree, ed., *Sources of Indian Tradition* (second edition) (New York: Columbia University Press, 1988) Vol. I p. 175-176.
94. Swami Sambuddhananda, *Vedānta Through Stories* (Bombay: Sri Ramakrishna Ashram, 1959) pp. 44-45.
95. A. Devaraja Mudaliar, compiler, *Gems From Bhagavan* (Tiruvannamalai:Sri Ramanasramam, 1985) p. 24-25.
96. Gopal Singh, *The Religion of the Sikhs* (Bombay: Asia Publishing House, 1971) p. 93-94.
97. *Talks With Sri Ramana Maharshi* (Tiruvannamalai: Sri Ramanasramam, 1984) p. 563.

98. *Ibid.*
99. William M. Indich, *Consciousness in Advaita Vedānta* (Delhi: Motilal Banarsidass, 1980) p. 65.
100. Paul Brunton, *Conscious Immortality* (Tiruvannamaalai: Sri Ramanasramam, 1984) p. 127.
101. *Ibid.*, p. 184.
102. M. Hiriyanna, *Essentials of Indian Philosophy*, p. 166.
103. *Ibid.*, p. 116.
104. A. Devaraja Mudaliar, compiler, *op. cit.*, p. 35.
105. Paul Brunton, *op. cit.*, p. 91.
106. David Godman, ed., *The Teachings of Sri Ramana Maharshi* (New York: Arkana, 1985) p. 53.
107. *Ibid.*, p. 52.
108. *Ibid.*
109. Swami Rajeswarananda, compiler, *Erase The Ego* (Bombay: Bharatiya Vidya Bhavan, 1974) p. 39.
110. A. Devaraja Mudaliar, compiler, *op. cit.*, p. 17.
111. Swami Rajeswarananda, compiler, *op. cit.*, p. 55.
112. Arthur Osborne, ed., *The Teachings of Bhagavan Ramana Maharshi in his Own Words* (Tiruvannamalai: T.N. Venkataraman, 1971) p. 249.
113. *Ibid.*, p. 228.
114. T.M.P. Mahadevan, tr., *Who Am I?* (Tiruvannamalai: Sri Ramanasramam, 1976) p. 2.
115. Sadhu Om, *The Path of Shri Ramana* (Kanpur: The City Book House, 1971) p. 28.
116. *Ibid.*, p. 32.
117. David Godman, ed., *op. cit.*, p. 158.
118. Sadhu Om, *op. cit.*, p. 26.
119. Sadhu Om, *op. cit.*, p. 46.
120. Swami Saradananda, *Sri Ramakrishna: The Great Master* (Madras: Ramakrishna Math, 1952) pp. 128-129.
121. B.V. Narsimha Swami, *Self-Realization: The Life and Teachings of Sri Ramana Maharishi.* (Tiruvannamalai: Sri Ramanasramam, 1985; first published 1931) p. 20.
122. Paul Brunton, *op. cit.*, p. 68.
123. J. Krishnamurti, *On Truth.* (San Francisco: Harper, 1995) pp. 24-29.
124. T.M.P. Mahadevan, *Outlines of Hinduism* (Bombay: Chetana Limited, 1971 [1956]) p. 141.
125. *Ibid.*

Bibliography

Basham, A.L. *The Wonder That Was India*, Rupa & Co, New Delhi, 1999 [1954].

Brunton, Paul. *Conscious Immortality*, Sri Ramanasramam, Tiruvannamalai, 1984.

Chatterjee, Satischandra, and Dhirendramohan Datta. *An Introduction to Indian Philosophy*, University of Calcutta, Calcutta, 1950.

De Bary., Wm. Theodore, Ed. *Sources of Chinese Tradition*, Columbia University Press, New York, 1960.

Edgertion, Franklin. "Studies in Veda", *Journal of the American Oriental Society*, 35: 242, 1915.

Embree, Ainslie T., Ed. *Sources of Indian Tradition* (second edition), Columbia University Press, New York, 1988.

Fort, Andrew O. *Jīvanmukti in Transformation: Embodied Liberation in Advaita and neo-Vedānta*, Albany, State University of New York Press, N.Y. 1998.

Frydman, Maurice, Tr. *I Am That: Conversations with Sri Nisaragadatta Maharaj*, Part I, Chetana, Bombay, 1973.

Godman, David, Ed. *The Teachings of Sri Raman Maharshi*, Arkana, New York, 1985.

Halbfass, Wilhelm. *India and Europe: An Essay in Understanding*, Albany, State University of New York Press, N. Y., 1988.

Hiriyanna, M. *Indian Philosophical Studies*, Kavyalaya Publishers, Mysore, 1957.

——. *The Essentials of Indian Philosophy*, George Allen & Unwin, London, 1949.

——. *Outlines of Indian Philosophy*, George Allen & Unwin, London, 1932.

Hopkins, Thomas J. *The Hindu Religious Tradition*, Encino, California and Belmont, Dickenson Publishing Company, California, 1971.

Hume, Robert Ernest. *The Thirteen Principal Upanishads*, Oxford University Press, London, 1968.

Hutchinson, John A. *Paths of Faith*, McGraw-Hill Book Company, New York, 1969.

Indich, William M. *Consciousness in Advaita Vedānta*, Motilal Banarsidass, Delhi, 1980.

Krishnamurti, J. *On Truth*, Harper, San Francisco, 1995.

Mahadevan, T. M. P., Tr. *Who Am I?* Sri Ramanasramam, Tiruvannamalai, 1976.

——. *Outlines of Hinduism*, Chetana Limited, Bombay, 1971 [1956].

——. *Talks With Sri Ramana Maharshi*, Sri Ramanasramam, Tiruvannamalai, 1984.

Mudaliar, A. Devaraj (compiler). *Gems From Bhagvan*, Sri Ramanasramam, Tiruvannamalai, 1985.

Murty, K. Satchidananda. *Revelation and Reason in Advaita Vedānta*, Motilal Banarsidass, Delhi, 1974.

Nicholson, Reynold A. *The Mystics of Islam*, Harmondsworth: Penguin, 1914 [1889].

Olivelle, Patrick. *The Early Upaniṣads*, Oxford University Press, New York, 1998.

Om, Sadhu. *The Path of Shri Ramana*, The City Book House, Kanpur, 1971.

Organ, Troy Wilson. *Hinduism: Its Historical Development*, Woodbury, Barron's Educational Series, N. Y., 1974.

Osborne, Arthur, Ed. *The Teachings of Bhagavan Ramana Maharshi in His Own Words*, T. N. Venkataraman, Tiruvannamalai, 1071.

Radhakrishnan, S. *The Principal Upaniṣads*, N. J.: Humanities Press, Atlantic Heights, 1992.

Swami Rajeswarananda (compiler). *Erase the Ego*. Bharatiya Vidya Bhavan, Bombay, 1974.

Swami Sambuddhananda. *Vedānta Through Stories*, Sri Ramakrishna Ashram, Bombay, 1959.

Sankaranarayanan, P. *What is Advaita?* Bharatiya Vidya Bhavan, Bombay, 1970.

Swami Saradananda, Tr. *Sri Ramakrishna: The Great Master*, Ramakrishna Math, Madras, 1952.

Sharma, Arvind. *The Philosophy of Religion and Advaita Vedānta: A Comparative Study in Religion and Reason*, The Pennsylvania State University Press, University Park, Pennsylvania, 1995.

Sharma, Chandradhar. *A Critical Survey of Indian Philosophy*, Rider, London, 1960.

Singh, Gopal. *The Religions of the Sikhs*, Asia Publishing House, Bombay, 1971.

Swami, B. V. Narasimha. *Self-Realization: The Life and Teachings of Sri Ramana Maharshi*, Sri Ramasramam Tiruvannamalai, 1985 [1931].

Zimmer, Heinrich. *Philosophies of India*, (Edited by Joseph Campbell), Princeton University Press, New York, 1969.

Index